"Kevin Adams writes with great richness, [writes with enormous Christian wisdom. E\ read this book."

—Cornelius Plantinga
Former president, Calvin Theological Seminary,
Author of *Not the Way It's Supposed to Be*

"Kevin Adams has written a gem of a book: one that renewed my love of the church, increased my respect for its imperfect-but-dedicated leaders, and bolstered my confidence in our ability to worship together across lines of significant difference. I laughed, winced in recognition, or nodded my head in agreement on every page. *The Gospel in a Handshake* should be required reading—not only for worship teams and pastors, but also the congregations that they serve."

—Melanie C. Ross
Associate Professor of Liturgical Studies, Yale Divinity School

"Kevin Adams is a veteran participant, observer, and professor of worship. If you find yourself desiring a fresh vision for worship and are kicking the tires of liturgy, sacrament, and the church calendar, you will find *The Gospel in a Handshake* a winning and winsome guide."

—Todd Hunter
Founding bishop, The Diocese of Churches for the Sake of Others

"Kevin Adams' wisdom is dispersed in these short but sweet letters to worship ministry leaders, both young and old alike. He brings encouragement, knowledge, and hope with a perfect balance of theology and pastoral advice in this book."

—Angie Hong
Worship leader, speaker, writer, urban liturgist

"Kevin Adams is a 'master carpenter' when it comes to the use of 'framing words' to help strengthen the worship life of any church. . . . *The Gospel in a Handshake* is a rich resource that will help build up a church and provide counsel to those called to lead and guide the worship mission ministry of the church."

—Jul Medenblik
President, Calvin Theological Seminary

"Worship is a public act—it is a corporate response to the public truth that Jesus is Lord. But many elements of Christian worship will seem strange to the new believer or those curious about Jesus. With clear wisdom and conversational warmth, Adams helps Christians understand and explain how worship is itself a way that we bear witness to the kingdom of God in the world around us."

—Glenn Packiam
Associate Senior Pastor, New Life Church
Author of *Blessed Broken Given: How Your Story Becomes Sacred in the Hands of Jesus*

The Gospel in a Handshake

WORSHIP AND WITNESS

The Worship and Witness series seeks to foster a rich, interdisciplinary conversation on the theology and practice of public worship, a conversation that will be integrative and expansive. Integrative, in that scholars and practitioners from a wide range of disciplines and ecclesial contexts will contribute studies that engage church and academy. Expansive, in that the series will engage voices from the global church and foreground crucial areas of inquiry for the vitality of public worship in the twenty-first century.

The Worship and Witness series demonstrates and cultivates the interaction of topics in worship studies with a range of crucial questions, topics, and insights drawn from other fields. These include the traditional disciplines of theology, history, and pastoral ministry—as well as cultural studies, political theology, spirituality, and music and the arts. The series focus will thus bridge church worship practices and the vital witness these practices nourish.

We are pleased that you have chosen to join us in this conversation, and we look forward to sharing this learning journey with you.

The Gospel in a Handshake

Framing Worship for Mission

KEVIN J. ADAMS

Foreword by Richard J. Mouw

CASCADE *Books* • Eugene, Oregon

THE GOSPEL IN A HANDSHAKE
Framing Worship for Mission

Worship and Witness

Cascade Books
An Imprint of Wipf and Stock Publishers
199 W. 8th Ave., Suite 3
Eugene, OR 97401

www.wipfandstock.com

PAPERBACK ISBN: 978-1-5326-9998-6
HARDCOVER ISBN: 978-1-5326-9999-3
EBOOK ISBN: 978-1-7252-4520-4

Cataloguing-in-Publication data:

Names: Adams, Kevin J., author.

Title: The gospel in a handshake: framing worship for mission / Kevin J. Adams.

Description: Eugene, OR: Cascade Books, 2019 | Series: Worship and Witness | Includes bibliographical references.

Identifiers: ISBN 978-1-5326-9998-6 (paperback) | ISBN 978-1-5326-9999-3 (hardcover) | ISBN 978-1-7252-4520-4 (ebook)

Subjects: LCSH: Public worship. | Christian Rituals and Practice—Worship and Liturgy. | Christian Rituals and Practice—General.

Classification: BV15 .A20 2019 (paperback) | BV15 (ebook)

Manufactured in the U.S.A.   12/09/19

To the good people of Granite Springs Church:
I am so grateful to belong to a congregation that loves and lives grace. Every day you invite people to bring their faith and doubt and to deepen their belief. Thanks for exploring together the art of framing worship for mission and for your patience along the way. You teach me about faith every day.

I rejoiced with those who said to me,
"Let us go to the house of the LORD."

—PSALM 122:1

Contents

Foreword

By Richard J. Mouw

THIS IS A MARVELOUS BOOK!

The emergence of the "worship leader" has been one of the significant liturgical developments of the past few decades. I see this as a good thing, and so does Kevin Adams. He wrote this fine book to provide counsel to those who are providing important leadership in worship.

We have always had various kinds of worship leaders in churches, of course. The congregations that my father served as a pastor could only support one ordained minister, but there were typically several "up front" persons giving leadership in our worship services. The organist. The choir director. And in our kinds of services, every Sunday evening there was the "song leader."

So, yes, in one sense there is nothing new about the role of worship leader. What distinguishes the present task of worship leader, however, is that person's relationship to yet another fairly recent innovation: "the worship team." And this "team" factor is significant, because it is linked to the widespread practice these days of worship *planning*. When I preach in a church with a worship team I typically am given a play-by-play sheet with projected time for each element of the service: Welcome, one minute; opening prayer, one minute; three songs, eleven minutes; and so on (including the clear signal that they will be watching to see how long I preach!).

Furthermore, the planning group has obviously reflected together about the integration of the various elements of the service. There is an effort made at a kind of thematic unity. This contrasts with the worship service of my youth. My dad was shocked one Sunday morning when the organist, who also did Saturday night gigs at the local skating rink (Hammond organs in both venues) played the tune to "Drink to me only with thine eyes, and

I'll not ask for wine," during the passing out of the communion elements. And our hymn sing leader, after asking for favorites from the congregation, would then instruct us to sing "the first, second, and fourth verses." Think of what it is like to go to verse four of "A Mighty Fortress" when you have skipped the previous verse.

For those of us with those memories, the emphasis these on planning for thematic unity in worship is a blessing. What is typically missing these days, though, is clarity about *liturgical* integrity. Words of welcome are a good thing, but why did the church of the past often require that a worship service begin with a "Salutation"? What did they mean by using that word, and why did it come to something more than (I heard this at a service recently) "Hi! I'm Mike and I want to tell you how glad I am that you are here today"?

Kevin cares deeply about these liturgical concerns, and he explores them in marvelous ways in these pages. He rightly sees the value of "time-tested" liturgical practices of the past, and he does an effective job of clarifying how they can come alive—albeit in new and creative ways—in contemporary worship.

He pursues his teaching task here by writing letters to a worship leader. I often find that books employing the "letters to" format to come across as a bit artificial. But not here. The informality of the friendly letter frees Kevin up to be offer some delightfully candid asides as he takes on some very practical issues that do not usually show up in books about worship. How do you handle a service on Mothers' Day and similar "Hallmark" events? What can we do to curb the kind of worship leader ad-libbing that actually undercuts—in some cases directly contradicts—the content of the sermon? How can we help visitors who have no idea what one is supposed to say when "passing the peace"? What about worship services that occur during times of civic holidays?

Kevin's letters comprise about two-thirds of this book, and he regularly makes his points by offering "frames"—examples of paragraph-long comments that show how to explain to a congregation the meaning of something that occurs in worship. His frames are impressively sensitive to cross-culture matters. Nor do they come across as elitist. He is not against contemporary relevance in worship. The important thing, he says, is to be "informed by the church of all ages" while making that wisdom "customized for your ZIP code."

After recording his letters to his worship leader friend, Kevin turns to a more systematic treatment of theological issues about worship. But here too his tone is lively and his observations are impressively practical in nature. While what he says here is valuable for all of us who study and teach about matters of worship, it is clear that he still sees his readership as including worship leaders and their teams.

Theological schools have been expanding their offerings in recent years to "nontraditional" students. But my hunch is that we are not going to see much by way of courses designed for worship leaders and praise groups. With books like this one available for them, however, we do not need to worry that the need is not being met. They can be inspired and informed by what Kevin offers to them here. And so can those of us who have much to learn from this book about how to engage in that teaching ministry.

Acknowledgments

DURING JUNIOR HIGH MY two younger brothers and I would attend two worship services each Sunday. The first, morning worship, bled immediately into Sunday school, after which we would meet the family at Grandma's home and debrief both events. A Sunday-sized dinner was then followed by a brief rest (no games or swimming or sports or even television for us) and then possibly youth choir practice, always a second worship service, and finally a youth group meeting. We called that litany of service-attending the "day of rest."

But an adolescent needs to grab sleep where he can, so along the way we mastered the art of propping a hymnbook between a knee and the pew in front of us and, so fixed in a (mostly) stationary position, we could "rest our eyes" while the pastor delivered his evening sermon, though occasionally our heads would bob us awake. (Even now in our congregation with movable chairs, engaging music, and inspiring sermons, I see similar strugglers, eyes resting and heads bobbing in a kind of churchy "amen.")

The worship order of those services decades ago was fixed. We never had any explanation or framing that I remember. Our congregation seemed to believe that sheer repetition would eventually bring meaning and purpose. My dad, a wonderful blue-collar believer, a school janitor for much of his later life, was himself a kind of convert to our congregation, making his (radical conversion) way from the Reformed denomination of his birth to the Reformed denomination of my mother's birth. Physically he converted, attending twice a Sunday. Internally he was in a state of mild rebellion to the somber, sober, serious worship of his adopted congregation.

I write this book for all of us who are still converting and still learning. All of us, secular and Christian, millennial and boomer, blue collar and highly educated, urban and suburban, are mere beginners at the invitation to worship. I hope these simple words will be an aid to those who worship and lead worship each week, and I ask your forgiveness for any that might be a hindrance. Much grace.

In writing this book I owe more thanks than I can express in a few lines, but let me acknowledge some:

To John Witvliet, who first conceived of this book and suggested I write it.

To faithful friends and readers of an early version of this manuscript who offered strategic, generous, and gracious advice that enhanced the book and kept me writing: Tim Blackmon, Angie Hong, and Jul Medenblik. A special thanks to my wife, Gerry, who gave invaluable suggestions and has been a joint worshiper and worship leader for all of our adult lives.

To Karen DeVries, a copy editor extraordinaire, who made insightful, strategic, and winning comments along the way. Her eye for detail made this book better at every turn.

To Michael Thomson and the other good people at Cascade Books.

To the people of Granite Springs Church: I am so grateful to belong to a congregation that loves and lives grace.

To the staff of the Calvin Institute of Christian Worship: these words are the fruit of your stellar work and love for congregations.

To those I have heard preach and sing and speak throughout a lifetime's worth of worship services, thank you for your work.

To all who have written and thought about and modeled worship framing: I have done my best to give you the credit you deserve. This is a project shared by many people and called by many names. We in the church learn from each other; my debt to you is great, and in many cases it is impossible to untangle our thinking. I am grateful to be pilgrims together in sharing gospel hope.

To the staff of Granite Springs Church: Thanks for being fellow pilgrims on the walk of faith. It is a gift to work with you, shoulder to shoulder, spreading grace.

To my wife, Gerry, and our adult children, Luke, Rachel, and J. J. The world is a much better place because of your presence in it. Thanks for your patience and kindness as I slipped away repeatedly to work on this project.

Introduction

On Framing a Book on Framing

AT THE CLOSE OF our Good Friday tenebrae service, a thoughtful reflection on Jesus' seven words on the cross in increasing and then final darkness, a soloist sang a cappella: "Were you there when they crucified my Lord?" It was touching and beautiful—a holy moment. With a few quiet final words, we encouraged everyone to reflect during what was left of Good Friday and through Holy Saturday on Jesus' love and suffering. To begin that reflection, we invited attendees to leave in silence. And they did. The soundless leave-taking of a typically boisterous group added to an already poignant moment.

When the ushers pushed open the doors for the silent gatherers to exit, a clear, distinct voice from the nursery greeted everyone: A wind-up toy at full volume got the final worship word: "The cow says 'moooo!'"

Really.

One Sunday morning, twenty minutes before the worship service, as we worship leaders focused on final preparations, the lights went out. Completely. At the time, we were meeting in a concrete warehouse with thirty-foot windowless walls. Suddenly and without warning, we were in the kind of utter darkness you usually experience in the depths of a subterranean cave. After a few moments of stunned disbelief, a mad scramble began. Several regulars raced home to retrieve camping lanterns. Another bolted to a nearby store to purchase batteries for a boom box that now would accompany our singing. Children's ministry workers speedily set up classrooms outside in the California sunshine.

At the exact moment everything was in place, fifteen minutes after our scheduled beginning, the power abruptly lurched back to life. Every electronic item in the building burst into high volume: speakers, fans, and lights all blared the news that the electricity was back. The lantern-lit vigil was abandoned.

Really.

Once, in that same warehouse during a special anniversary worship service, we were celebrating communion. We had sung favorite songs, told stories of God's goodness and grace, and rehearsed personal and communal life change. Our surroundings were humble, but clearly the Holy Spirit was working, restoring, and renewing many. This was exactly the kind of life change we dared hope would happen years before when we launched the congregation. Overwhelmed by the words of the evening, I was nearly overcome with emotion. Thankfully I mustered enough composure to lead the liturgy, eventually uttering the familiar words, "The blood of Christ, shed for you."

At that exact moment, a bat swooped from the upper recesses of our sanctuary, soaring inches over attendees' heads. It darted and dove, soared and sailed, hovered and floated. We knew it lived nearby; we were used to seeing guano on top of our audiovisual screen or on the carpet. But it chose that nanosecond for an inaugural visit—a dazzling display of aeronautical introduction.

Really.

If we were sitting together in a café and you showed the slightest interest in these stories, I'd regale you with more, like the time a guest preacher took too long to end his sermon. Just as restless as the human listeners, but a bit less polite, a field mouse darted toward the completely unaware preacher, who was engulfed in his own oration. Sitting in the front row and not knowing what else to do (no worship class prepared me to shepherd church mice), I tapped my shoe toward the pink-tailed attendee in a nonverbal "Shoo!" It got the message. Its muscle reflex sent him to the back of the platform, out of sight. But the sermon continued, and every few minutes the religious rodent returned, determined to get the attention of our speaker and the entire congregation. And so began, in this sermon that wouldn't end, a verbal shoe and mouse game.

I might also recount the morning a recently released convict attended for the first time and gave his own impromptu call to worship. He had been corresponding with a staff member who had recently taken a job in another town. No one in the building knew him, nor were we prepared to meet his request, even when he bellowed it at full volume as our service began, "Someone needs to buy me a car right now or something bad will happen!" I was never more thankful for skillful ushers built like linebackers, one a therapist with prison experience.

I could tell you about the Sunday mornings when the heater didn't work, and we bundled up in a forty-five-degree room. Or days we sat amid buckets strategically placed between chairs to catch steady drips from a leaking roof. Or the time a new attendee, looking like an Old Testament prophet, announced in a series of intense post-worship conversations: "They are not preaching the gospel here." Or the worship service when one of our volunteer Scripture readers, growing more and more uncomfortable with his assigned reading, grabbed the flashlight meant to help him read in the dim sanctuary, lit up his face in the shadowy way of a Halloween jack-o'-lantern, and began his reading with a ghoulish, menacing "Hellooo."

Really.

The task of planning and leading worship is unpredictable and humbling. On one hand all Christian worship, whether held in a dilapidated warehouse, a medieval cathedral, or on a Hawaiian beach, joins us with the angel choruses and the great cloud of witnesses. All worship leading is informed by what's happening in heaven. We have one eye on the ever-singing angels who behold God's glory and our desire to meet the Holy One. But it's also true, as we know fearfully well, that our worship leading happens here on earth—at least for now. So no matter our skill or expertise or preparation, we focus another eye on what's in front of us, and that can be acutely ordinary. No wonder the Apostle Paul tells the Corinthian church that ministry will always have both glory and dishonor.

The moments when hearts lift to a soaring doxology played by a talented string quartet or offer a tender prayer on a recent pastoral issue seem equally matched by times a featured cantor gets a head cold or a scheduled Scripture reader's child gets the flu and texts an apology a minute before the service begins. One week in the midst of worship, you might uncover the baptismal font to find someone has forgotten to place water inside. The next moment, a toddler in a moment of unexpected baptismal tenderness tucks his head close to your chest as you read the oft-repeated formula. One Sunday you feel as if everything and everyone was out of sync; another Sunday you baptize radiant adults and children.

In the ongoing realities we face, we are colleagues with each other, with all who have gone before, and with those who will take our place—all of us called to this wonderful and wonderfully humbling task of leading worship. It's not enough that you pray and plan and listen to the Holy Spirit; you also work with imperfect people and fluctuating situations. Ailments ruin best laid plans. A sparrow tangles with a key electrical circuit. An ill-timed cell phone rings just before the sermon's closing line—and the recipient answers. You work regularly with competing expectations and petty rivalries, some that you've unfortunately helped create and others you inherit. And that's just for folks who already attend. Add the mission-minded expectation that, in all the tedium and glory of an ordinary worship service, a spiritually seeking novice to church needs to understand and even be captivated by worship. These nagging expectations, spoken and unspoken, stagger the most stout-hearted leader. Who wouldn't give up and walk away?

Aware of the never-ending challenge of your task, I hope this book is a gift. It is designed to support you in the very practical circumstances and challenges of your week-to-week worship leading. We all need help, and most of us need it regularly.

I also hope you will let your worship planning and leading be guided, informed, and even inspired by the church of all times and places. The church has many treasures, and its worship life embodies many of them.

Throughout what follows, in the form of letters to a new worship leader, you'll hear bits and pieces of our congregation's journey from what we now recognize as a particularly North American evangelical pattern of worship to the historic ecumenical liturgy. For its first ten years, our congregation incorporated weekly dramas, children's messages, and guest soloists accompanied by boom boxes in emergencies. We worked hard every week to be creative and capture interest. And we were good at it —most days. No one said so explicitly, but we thought it our task to create spiritual curiosity through innovation. The mission-oriented people I trusted most believed that to reach secular or skeptical people with the gospel, to make the biggest possible difference in their neighborhood, ministry leaders needed to leave the ineffective worship ways of the past, to exchange the old-fashioned stuff for something more relevant and helpful to mission.

As far as I remember, no one wrote a white paper on this idea. No one proved it empirically. It was just something everyone knew. Twenty-eight years and many conversations later, I now know everyone knew this because so many of us are shaped by the thinking and practice of leaders like George Whitefield and Charles Finney and so much of what we call American evangelicalism. But we didn't know it back then.

So our congregation did what everyone knew would work. And it did. They came—people from an astonishing variety of spiritual backgrounds, and many without any church experience as adults. I had never been part of a church like that before.

But in those early years, whenever I attended a more traditional worship service, I found myself yearning to participate in many of its elements. I wasn't sure why. Was it nostalgia? Did I yearn for much-loved hymns only because they stirred sentiments in me from my adolescence? Did I only treasure these worship elements because I could imagine my grandparents engaging in them? Possibly. But now I think there was something else going on. Something deeper. Something mission-oriented.

Now we know that we didn't need to choose between the timeless elements of Christian worship and mission. The archetypal elements, even the less familiar ones, overflow with it. This makes sense. All worship reorients us and deepens our connection to the God of mission. Instead of feeling constant pressure to capture the interest and attention of secular people each week through endless creativity and innovation, we now trust the liturgy's timeless message of grace to offer its built-in gospel intrigue. As worship leaders, we might say we experience grace even as we speak about grace.

A key to experiencing mission in the time-tested liturgy—or any worship framework, for that matter—is real-world hospitality. That may not feel like earth-shattering news. But the challenge is in the details. It's one thing to talk about hospitality, and another to do it well. Our hospitality through the years has often been clumsy. It's painful when someone trusts us enough to bring a skeptical brother-in-law or spiritually agnostic boss to worship only to have us say something unintentionally or thoughtlessly off-putting.

The aim of this book is to help worship leaders skillfully guide spiritual novices, skeptics, and yes, Christian veterans, to the grace embedded in the liturgy and the liturgical year. You'll find lots of hospitality specifics in the following pages. Much of that worship hospitality will be in the form of what we might call "in-between words." You'll read a lot of pithy introductions we'll call "frames" that alert attendees to the character and purpose of various worship elements. And you'll get the tools to create your own framework, informed by the church of all ages but customized for your ZIP code. To employ these words as simple worship cues is to engage in what a friend calls "liturgy by explanation." Strategically used and winsomely done, they can help novices and veterans see the gospel's beauty.

I've shaped these thoughts on worship hospitality as a series of letters. I've imagined I'm writing to a novice worship leader and a new worship team navigating their first year of leading a local congregation in worship. You might say the letters were written to my younger self. But they're also for worship leaders who are leading a new church, a campus ministry, or a congregation actively seeking renewal, those who might have experts and well-intentioned leaders around them saying, "You can't reach secular people with that old content and those old ways."

The letters are also written for people like the wonderful attendees of the first congregation I had the joy to pastor, the good people in small-town Minnesota who welcomed these ideas. When we first talked about offering hospitality in this way they might have protested, "Why work so hard at this when we don't have any spiritual novices in our church?" But instead we kept working together, learning to be hospitable by talking to the empty seats. It was a full two years of using hospitable and welcoming language before anyone dared to bring a friend. But eventually they did.

Really.

The letters show a kind of trajectory. Along the way, it's been my pleasure to teach worship and to listen to students, interns, and other friends who trust the beauty and grace of the church's time-tested liturgy and want to help others see its grace as well. None of us is an expert. We don't need to be. We walk this path together, learning as we go. As you read, I hope you'll feel the mutual respect, the sense of easy conversation between friends who trust and support each other, and a taste of the kind of community where conversations aim for grace and truth. And I hope you'll surpass these examples.

The letters are arranged to follow a first year in parish ministry, with a summer correspondence outlined around the basic shape of a worship service. Following them you'll find a brief section that's more didactic, offering wisdom to help readers see and develop a kind of worship philosophy. The book concludes with a ready index of worship frames by topic. Some weeks, what we need is ready-made help. But first, a year's (and more) worth of letters for anyone who wants to increasingly offer worship hospitality and heighten their congregation's mission IQ.

Really.

Kevin Adams
Trinity Sunday, 2019

P.S. One more word about worship. I believe, even in the erratic, seemingly random, and unwanted tedium of actual week-to-week services, that worship is a doorway to grace. The bulk of a congregation's pastoral care, identity formation, and spiritual growth happen or can happen in worship. In worship we learn about ourselves and our God (and in learning about our God, learn even more about ourselves). In worship we learn that our own lives are not our own or even fundamentally about us, but that we belong to another, the one to whom we pray, "Our Father in heaven, hallowed be your name."

PART ONE

Letters

"You have made us for yourself, O Lord, and our heart is restless until it rests in you."

—Augustine (Confessions)

"You make known to me the path of life; you will fill me with joy in your presence, with eternal pleasures at your right hand."

Psalm 16:11 (NIV)

September

On Saying Yes: Our Inadequacy and the Call of God

Dear Jordan,

I can't begin to tell you how delighted I am that you and your friends have taken on the worship leadership of your church. You'll be terrific. You're thoughtful, wise, humble, and best of all, you love God deeply. That love, so contagious and full of life, will draw people more deeply into worship, both those who already worship regularly at your congregation and the spiritual skeptics and curious in the neighborhood around you.

Thanks for sharing your sense of inadequacy about this new position. I completely agree with you. And I mean this in the most loving way: you are exactly right—you are decidedly *not* qualified to lead worship. (I hope you didn't think I'd *dis*agree with you.) But take heart; no one is.

Still, when God calls—in your case, through the still, small voice of a new pastor—we dare to answer "yes." Not because we're able. Not because we're ready. Not because you have up-front gifts or any other kind of qualification. And not even because you've had stellar theological training, though those of us who teach in such settings and subjects hope such experience will be an aid and not a hindrance! None of us is qualified. Who of us can know enough or presume enough to lead people into the presence of God? It's not clichéd to say that no one is fit to lead worship.

Don't stress too much that you have only three weeks to prepare for the launch of the upcoming church year. Your life overflows with experiences that will enable you to be a good leader. Your (brief) study of theology will help. So will your musical acumen. Equally important will be your character. Your humility and teachable spirit will be invaluable as you step into a role no one is ever fully prepared to take. Experience is a fine teacher, sure to give wisdom to those who pay attention. And yes, of course, I'm glad to chat weekly during this, your first year.

Still, it's only fair to warn you: it's a dangerous business. A friend of mine, a Roman Catholic priest, once talked about priests with "singed hands." They've touched the mystery of Eucharist so often they no longer seem able to experience the miracle of grace. It's as if repeating the mystery inoculated them from what they offer others. My friend's image speaks to the danger of taking our call to lead worship for granted. We all know people of every era and church network who seem to sleepwalk through services, even ones they lead. It's tempting (and this temptation increases over time, I'm afraid) to skim, to shrink the task of worship planning to an emotional bandwidth that makes us reasonably comfortable.

But it's also holy work. Because you've said yes to this, your life will never be the same. Your faith will be challenged, your sensitive heart will be toughened, and your convictions about what matters and what doesn't will deepen. It makes me think of that old aphorism that a pastor needs the mind of a scholar, the heart of a child, and the hide of a rhinoceros. All in due time. Like all God's prophets, priests, and kings before you, you're off on a huge adventure, and you'll be richer for it.

This "yes" will change your life forever—and by God's grace, the lives of many others too.

How wonderful!

Kevin

Worship Wars: On Not Seeing Eye to Eye (Gracefully)

Dear Jordan,

So your team is already in turmoil. Half want a cool, hip band, and half want something simple and elegant. Some want full amplification; some want natural acoustics. Some want well-known and much-loved hymns of the faith; some are determined to support the artistry of home-grown talent. Everyone seems determined to fight adamantly for their position and threaten to walk out if others don't agree. And that was just the first ten minutes of your meeting!

And that's just within your worship planning group. Already longtime congregants are questioning why the pastor asked you—*you*, of all people— to lead. You lack experience, they say, and wisdom. And you don't know the congregation well enough. Some are threatening to leave; others arrive at church only after the music is over. Of course. So it is. And so it might always be.

I'm not surprised by emotionally charged opinions about worship. I hope you won't be either. Worship touches the deepest part of us. It's hard to think rationally when we talk about the language of our soul. That your team already seemed on the verge of splitting in only your second meeting (you're right that no amount of pizza can bring divergent worship ideas into harmony) isn't necessarily something to cause panic. It was not for dramatic effect that one of my seminary professors dubbed worship the "war department" of the church. People divide worship in all sorts of ways, using titles and terms that separate and polarize. Many you heard at your meeting last night: contemporary vs. traditional, attractional vs. missional, high decibel vs. contemplative, guitar-driven vs. piano-led, praise team vs. organ. People separate worshipers by age and denomination and heritage. Several church growth experts told me the way to guarantee growth in a congregation is to have no up-front music leaders over thirty years old. I hope you won't follow that bad, if in some settings also effective, advice.

One way through all this (and trust me, there's no magic bullet or quick fix) is to build a common vocabulary or language for speaking about worship. One book I've found helpful is *Evangelical versus Liturgical?: Defying a Dichotomy*, by Melanie C. Ross.

It's terrific: gentle and helpful, generous and engaging. Ross includes vibrant examples of specific congregations working to worship in ways both timeless and specific to their contexts. In her book, she outlines two main worship patterns (therefore the term *dichotomy*) at work in North America. Both come with enthusiastic, even passionate practitioners. And many of these practitioners have the built-in assumption that following their pattern is the only true way forward. It's worth reading the book, if only to hear what Ross says in her introduction and the first chapter. It will especially help attendees with deep convictions about what should and should not be included in worship even if they don't know the exact source of their convictions or passion.

I can hear my church history professor laughing. How many times did one of his lectures remind us that for lack of knowing history we charge ahead, full of principles and enthusiasm, convinced we've invented some novel way to cure the church from all that ails, when all along the shape of that bright idea came from something we inherited from generations before us. Most lead worship with an unconscious "order" in their head and heart. They sense it's been handed down to them, but they're not sure where it came from. This happens in every kind of church, both formal and informal.

What if you read Ross's book? Then we'll talk again.

In the meantime, I wish you grace in the midst of relational conflict. This is no time to wave around your degree, nor is it time to play the expert.

Be gentle and understanding. Many of these folks were part of that congregation before you were born. Listen well. See God's face in each other. Dare to go on a journey together, even one without an exact destination. Come to think of it, maybe you all want to read that book together?

> Much grace,
> Kevin

On Liturgical Architecture and Worship Components

Dear Jordan,

I'm glad you liked the book, and that many on your team did too. No, I wasn't surprised a few found it a little "deep" or technical for their taste. But with you I celebrate that they gained an orientation and understanding of favorite, if often subconscious, patterns in North American worship.

Of course, some people resonated with the fourfold *ordo*, the shape of Christian liturgy that has guided Christians since the second century: bath, word, table, sending. To worship in this way is to worship in ways that connect to Christians of all times and places. It's ecumenical, transcending era and context. As you said, many on your team will support this outline because it's the pattern they've most experienced in the past. Others will be drawn to it simply because it's the main practice of the church for all times and places. Still, it's not at all surprising, given your North American context, that others resonated with what Ross calls the three-part "frontier ordo": warm-up, sermon, and call to conversion.[1]

Maybe there's a way to learn from each other?

You know enough of our congregation's story to know that for more than ten years we (without being conscious of these two options) practiced the frontier ordo. Like those who intuitively shaped this order, we rejected the historic ecumenical practice as too stuffy, formal, and predictable. With many others, we labeled it dated, unable to capture the imagination and interest of those exploring the faith. And by God's good grace, many people came to faith in our congregation. More than we dared hope, actually. It's hard to argue with the effectiveness of Charles Finney, George Whitefield, or Billy Graham.

The truth is that in those early years we had precious little idea of how to start a congregation. We believed we needed to start a custom worship service especially suited to our neighborhood. So we did. It's ironic that our years of innovative drama, creative children's messages, and winning

---

1. Ross, *Evangelical versus Liturgical?*, 3

music style were really following an ordo we had never heard described or explained. That's why I support (and urge you to support) Ross's call to generosity here. Your congregation will need to decide what direction to go. Will you follow one of these two guides? Will you try to do something customized and original?

What do *I* recommend?

I think you should decide.

I can hear you protesting from where I type! Sure, maybe my answer feels like a cop-out. But I push your question back to you because there's great temptation to have conversations like this framed by guilt ("If you don't do it like me, be *shamed*") and fear ("Worship practices like yours lead to *shallow* congregations") and pride ("We're so glad we don't worship like those *half-witted* novices").[2] Let the gospel shape worship, and let the gospel be the good news it is.

Still, you asked an honest question. So here's an honest answer: you can't do much better than a liturgy used for two thousand years. The endlessly quotable and insightful British newspaperman and author G. K. Chesterton put it this way: "Tradition refuses to submit to the small and arrogant oligarchy of those who merely happen to be walking about."[3] I find this lived-in the life and ministry of my friend Chris, a Greek Orthodox priest. His church uses a liturgy from the fourth century. Once, as the two of us were leaving a conference for and by (mostly Protestant) worship leaders, I asked him his impression. His response echoes in me still today: he felt sorry for people who feel pressure to be innovative every week. It seemed such a burden—an unnecessary burden for a timeless community that already has a life-giving liturgy. We can't do much better than a liturgy used for two thousand years. My underlying conviction and hope is that winsomely framing this treasured liturgy in a way that directly engages unbelievers who are always present unveils its gospel grace for a new generation of believers. But I bet you already knew I was going to say that!

Much grace,
Kevin

2. Ross, *Evangelical versus Liturgical?*, 4.
3. Chesterton, *Orthodoxy*, 85.

On Designing Worship "Moments," or Trusting the Slowness of Historic Worship

Dear Jordan,

I know. There's a strong pull in congregations to create worship "moments." There's an expectation among many attendees that these must happen weekly—or more.

From your letter, it sounds as if many in your congregation carry this expectation inside—and with passionate conviction. One reason many congregations hire high quality, captivating musical performers is they believe such people can most optimally meet this expectation. They can *move* worshipers.

You're saying that many people in your congregation want to *know* they've been in the presence of God during a worship service. Part of this is wonderful: they worship with a sense of anticipation about meeting God. But most of us who've led worship have our own version of your story about the enthusiastic attendee who greets her friends as they leave the building with, "What did you think of today's worship?" It's as if there's a scale for rating worship like a reviewer rates a new movie with one to four stars. In a world where people rate restaurants and coffee shops, nail salons and dog groomers (all with the same app!), it's tempting to feel or succumb to the pressure to make every Sunday an *experience*.

Obviously this is not a plea or excuse for mediocrity. And knowing you like I do, I know you're committed to well-prepared music and prayerful worship leading. But once you yield to the expectation—whether from inside you or within your church culture—that every worship service includes sparkling innovation, you've put yourself on a treadmill you can't easily get off. Many congregations shaped and formed spiritually by such an unending and relentless weekly quest for novelty end up losing sight of gospel grace. In such venues, every worship service needs to be ever increasing in experiential voltage. Creating experiences becomes your job, and that of your team. Such moments become your main task.

Even if you are able to create such moments, is such an ever-escalating succession of Sundays in the best interest of the worshipers who demand it? Or of your worship team? Is such ever increasing emotional voltage even good for your congregation? And is creating worship experiences really your job? Is that good for your soul? While we want our friends attending for the first time to be captivated during worship at our church and to return with enthusiasm and expectation, the deepest effect of worship happens over time.

One way we say it at our church is that worship is *slow*.

We don't mean the pace of our music is slow or that the sermons drag on. But we believe that because God welcomes us exactly as we are, and because God does not often transform lives all at once, we who lead worship can be patient. As you design worship, I'd encourage your team to be more interested in what happens during fifty-two services that practice the timeless and transforming rhythms of worship than creating a single exciting spiritual experience. (In our congregation, fifty-two Sundays represents a four- or even ten-year total of Sunday attendance for many.)

High-voltage, life-changing experiences have their place. But if mission is your goal, it happens just as naturally in the historic practices of the church week to week as in a novel service orchestrated to be emotionally moving.[4]

A few years ago, we had a service in which we remembered our baptisms. Following the practice of our Eastern Orthodox friends, we dipped a branch (they use hyssop, we used redwood for a particularly Californian flavor) into a bowl and walked throughout the congregation, sprinkling attendees and saying, "In baptism God tells you: 'You are my beloved child.'" One woman, attending her third service, told me afterward, "When the water hit, it was the biggest high of my life. Higher than my previous trips from marijuana or acid or booze or sex. It was like I levitated. Like the Holy Spirit healed me and made me whole."

And to think that morning I felt anxiety about trying that ancient practice for the first time, wondering how our congregation, and especially newer attendees, would experience it. You never know what's going to happen on a Sunday morning. As one of my mentors frequently says, "Another name for God is *Surprise*."

Here's to God surprising us,
Kevin

On the Value of Historic Liturgy
for Multicultural Congregations

Dear Jordan,

I'm not surprised you're getting pushback on your resolve (insistence?) to let the time-tested historic elements of ecumenical worship lead and form you and your congregation in worship. There's no doubt these classic elements

---

4. Thanks to Matt Timms who first named this idea "slow worship" in our congregation.

will seem terribly old-fashioned to more than a few. Those who think (and feel) that way have a lot of company. They have good, earnest, deeply Christian company. Still, like you, I'm more and more convinced the time-tested elements will serve your congregation well, both spiritual veterans and novices.

Thanks for asking about your group's protest that the classic ordo is less than optimal for a congregation with a variety of ethnic and economic backgrounds. The reaction you relayed, about the several team members who argued "This classic worship format is only suited for college-educated, majority-culture folks!" isn't surprising. I've heard it too. It's wise to listen to those voices. With you, I celebrate the diversity of your team. To have people from a constellation of backgrounds and worship experiences is a gift to each of you and your church as a whole. It will help you move beyond what is parochial and the preferences of a few. And the recent immigrants you described add a wonderful sense of the global identity of the church. It's one thing to confess that in Christ "there is no Gentile or Jew, circumcised or uncircumcised, barbarian, Scythian, slave or free."[5] It's something completely different and magnificent and complicated to experience it week after messy week.

Still, it might help your group to know that the ecumenical order you are using is the most-used worship framework in the entire history of the church. The great majority of congregations in Africa, Asia, Europe, and the Americas worship in the same way you do. Your worship isn't specific to an ethnic group or social class; it is transcultural, transdenominational, and panethnic. Most of the church in all times and places has worshipped like you. That includes Augustine and Athanasius (North Africa) and Bishop Tutu (South Africa). It includes Francis of Assisi and King Olaf (Europe), Jonathan Edwards and Dorothy Day (North America), Jeanette Li and Cheng Jingyi (Asia), Oscar Romero and Pope Francis (South and Central America). On and on goes the list.

I won't press the point. You get the idea. And I hope the rest of your team will be open to this historical reality as well: the ecumenical ordo you are using is exactly what stretches your congregation beyond what is culturally immediate, merely contextual, or monogenerational. Most of the church, in most languages in most ethnic groups, in most economic situations, in most of the history of the world have worshiped in this way. And today most Christians, including the poorest of the poor, worship in this way. It's important to clarify and state this reality.

5. Col 3:11, NIV.

Our conversation makes me think of my friend Scot. Scot loves liturgy with the same passion he loves a fine cigar, a vintage bottle of wine, and an Italian opera. From the outside, he seems an exact fit for the category of well educated and verbally adroit persons some claim are most suited to the classic worship outline. But the classic liturgy of the church, like a favorite beverage or music choices, transcends categories. Scot first learned this while serving in a working-class Philadelphia church. Each week the opening line of the liturgy sounded as if it were being recited by Rocky Balboa:

"The Lord be wit you."

"And also wit you!"

Much grace,
Kevin

October

On Mission-Shaped Historic Liturgy and Needing Grace

Dear Jordan,

The protests continue?

Maybe if you think of these taxing, heated dialogues less as verbal combat and more as spiritual formation exercises you can be a bit less anxious about them? I know, easier said than done. Or *felt*. And it's clear from your letter that you're feeling some trepidation about all this. Okay, a lot of fear, even dread, and the sleepless nights that go with it! But be of good cheer: good leaders know it can be advantageous for team members to have divergent opinions. The important thing is to express them with love and respect and then to implement your joint plans in unity.

I hope you are also feeling you're making headway. There's a lot of learning happening. It's heartening to read that your group now realizes that most Christians, regardless of ethnic group or language, have used the elements of the classic liturgy. That itself is no small point of agreement. But now their concern is that such a classic liturgy is not suited to the spiritual novices and skeptics? Salute them! That's exactly the question you'd want your leadership group to ask!

I remember a veteran church attendee in the first days of our church asking the same question in a different way. We had a congregation full of people with a dazzling tapestry of spiritual backgrounds—Buddhist, Hindu, agnostic, atheist, and many breeds of Christian. Reflecting on the diverse attendees, the churchgoer asked, "Once the congregation 'grows up' and you no longer have spiritual novices inside the church, you'll change to a more mature kind of worship, right?"

The assumption by both my friend and some in your group is that there's one kind of worship service most helpful to novices and another ideal for spiritual veterans. But what we've found in our congregation is consistent with what others have experienced around the world: the timeless worship service has everything needed for every kind of spiritual reality or experience.

Let's see if I can clarify the issue with some questions. What kind of person most needs a weekly confession? What kind of person needs weekly Eucharist? What kind of person most benefits from a gospel sermon? Or a reminder of baptismal identity? Or a weekly blessing? Each of these worship elements brings a specific kind of grace. And doesn't each and every attendee of each and every spiritual background need those specific graces *every* week?

More later,
Kevin

On Frames for Worship: In-Between Words and Missional Cues

Dear Jordan,

What's helpful is to introduce various historic worship elements in a way that clarifies their beauty and purpose for all attendees. As an act of hospitality, we introduce the components of our worship service with a few words of explanation. In worship planning we talk about these simple introductions as *frames*.

Think of the worship elements as treasures in an art gallery. Frames around these treasures can be thin or thick, timeless or contemporary, indigenous or imported. Each is designed to highlight what guests come to see in the gallery: the treasures. Frames can change or be replaced. Good ones help you see and understand the Picasso or Rembrandt or Pollock.

Have you ever been to a great art gallery and taken a tour? A skillful guide doesn't spend the entire tour merely talking, but helps guests see and discover for themselves. She gives cues like "Look for this color," or offers something to seek, like "Find the artist's inconsistent brushstrokes." She may offer historical perspective like "Imagine which painting was early in his career and which was later," or compare and contrast, such as "Notice how these artists use light in the same way."

A few years ago, our family took a tour of Westminster Abbey. We were in awe simply to be there in London! We could hardly believe our good fortune. And the Abbey is quite impressive, of course. To think Christians have worshiped at the site for 1,400 years! But it was also overwhelming, especially to us novices—not only because they speak an unfamiliar kind of English, but more because the Abbey is packed with an vast array of grave markers, memorial plaques, monuments, and medieval treasures. Being largely unfamiliar with British history only deepened our fog of bewildered overstimulation.

But then we met Benjamin. For two hours, Benjamin, an Abbey verger, served as our tour guide. With disarming grace and wit, he led us through the Abbey, pausing to tell a quick story or stopping to point out a treasure. He knew when to speak and when to provide moments for us to explore on our own. He included the children and connected with guests from multiple countries, dodging artfully as he led the group between slow-moving tourists and answering questions he must have heard a hundred times before with charm and genuine interest. Ten years later our family still considers that tour a top family memory and Benjamin, whom we only knew for those two hours, a lifelong friend. It didn't hurt that he got us seats in the choir loft for the evensong service!

We've had other tour guides in various settings: San Francisco art galleries, national monuments, Welsh castles, giant panda exhibits, and underground caves. Some guides were repetitive robots, some self-absorbed blabbers, others information geeks that buried us in an avalanche of unhelpful details. But Benjamin had the ability to frame something in a way we could understand and absorb. We'll treasure that experience always.

Worship leaders aren't tour guides exactly (more on that later), but we can help people experience the timeless treasures of the faith in a similar way. Our "in-between words" can offer cues that help people see what they came to see: the treasures of grace.

Last week a seminary student wrote a blog post for the worship class I teach. A lifelong church attendee, he was in a theology class learning about the elements of worship and their purpose. In the post he asked, "Why didn't someone explain these elements so I understood them? As a child growing up I had no idea of their treasure."

In the early days of our church we tossed out many of the classic worship elements—the call to worship, confession, benediction—because we judged them irrelevant and confusing to people new or lukewarm to the faith. What we found over time is that the problem wasn't with the elements, but with how we as worship leaders framed them. We aimed to be hospitable, but our hospitality actually reduced attendees' experience of grace.

It makes me think of the quote from G. K. Chesterton, who wrote to what was a very churched and culturally Christian Britain at the time, "The Christian ideal has not been tried and found wanting. It has been found difficult; and left untried."[1]

---

1. Chesterton, *What's Wrong with the World*, ch. 1.

If you ever get a chance to visit Westminster, take a tour—and ask for Benjamin.

More later,
Kevin

On Maps, Being Lost, and Worship Leading as Wayfinding

Dear Jordan,

As a bonus this week (I do hope you'll think it's a bonus and not a burden), I want to send a follow-up note to our discussion about worship frames. The metaphor works when we think of a place like Westminster Abbey, or the Metropolitan Museum of Art, or the wall of photographs in Grandma's hallway. But after I sent the last note, I wondered if the framing metaphor might not be optimal in every context.

Worship in a church doesn't always feel like an art gallery. For many it feels like a foreign country where even the directional signs are in an unfamiliar language.

On that same family trip to Europe, we stayed a week in France. Thanks to a generous church attendee, we spent a lovely week in a cottage near a small town in the French countryside. A friend had told me that it's worth going to France simply to breathe the air, lunch on cheese and wine, and eat a fresh pastry for breakfast. He was absolutely right. And it's worth going to church to hear the words of an old hymn or to receive a blessing. But it turns out you can't experience those things without a map.

Our family of five navigated France armed only with my son's high school French. Often we were disoriented. Or completely lost. We spent half an hour in a Paris subway waiting for a train, only to learn through a kind bystander's halting and reluctant English that the train we wanted would arrive two floors down. Once on the proper train, we squashed into narrow seats with luggage for five, only to have an upset fellow subway patron become visibly and demonstrably irate with us for breaking an obvious code of subway travel. She hissed and bellowed at us in rapid-fire French, and then to her boyfriend as well. We easily interpreted her body language and verbal tone, but since we couldn't understand any of her words, we had no idea what to change about our behavior to ease her pain or to get in line with cultural mores. (Think of a first-time worship attendee who doesn't know she's sitting in someone's seat!)

Another afternoon we carefully followed a train attendant's painstaking instructions to catch the only train that would take us to the famous cathedral city of Chartres. Finding it odd to be the only passengers on a particular side of the tracks, we reassured ourselves by rehearsing what we took to be the attendant's repeated instructions. When the train stopped on the other side of the tracks, one passenger smirked our way before getting on, nodding to our American clothes. With a mix between a grin and a sneer, he said for all in that modest train station to hear, "Vive la France." Sometimes going to church can be as disorienting (and unfriendly) as a French train station.

In such cases, imagine worship leading as the work of wayfinding. Expert wayfinders pay careful attention to the placement of signs and images and even words that function as signs. They point the way, helping novices navigate the uncharted territory of worship.

Novice worshipers want to know where they are located in the universe, in the grand scheme of things, but also right now in worship. Wayfinding not only helps people navigate the liturgy, it also challenges them to think through life's route decisions that worship will prompt them to make. The idea of wayfinding helps us see worship as a way of life.

Professional wayfinders structure airports and city centers so people from a wide variety of languages, ages, and physical abilities can navigate successfully to their proper destinations. They identify possible barriers to navigation and work to remove them. Isn't the same true for worship leaders?

Wayfinding has to do with giving the right directions at the right time for the right people. Christian worship is uncharted territory for secular people. To make worship intelligible and to make active, fully conscious participation possible, someone needs to create a map.

A few years ago, two college freshman from our congregation visited a new city while on a weekend trip with their college suitemates. While the majority of their fellow travelers slept in that Sunday morning, recovering from Saturday night adventure, these two got up early (at least for college students) and found the nearest church. (I like to think their godly behavior was a direct result of the excellent spiritual formation they received from our church youth group. But it's just as likely they needed coffee.) When it came time for the Eucharist, they stepped into the line moving forward, just like at home with us. At the communion rail, the priest offered "The body of Christ for you." The first of our young congregants, following the pattern of many church traditions, responded "Thanks be to God" and was given the host and chalice. The second, immediately behind him but paying less attention to the repeated words of other worshipers, said offhandedly and instinctively, "Thank you very much."

We might argue it's a remarkable act of faith for any college freshman to attend a Sunday morning worship service. We might also argue that such a godly act should allow one to fully participate in this means of grace. But his unorthodox words prompted the priest to quickly and deftly pull back the host and instead offer him a blessing. One young lad had a kind of internal wayfinder. The other needed direction.

Couldn't every worshiper, novice and veteran, benefit from a kind of map for moving forward?

Again, it's not so much the metaphor or image that's important; what matters is the grace-filled hospitality.[2]

Yours,
Kevin

On Mission-Shaped Frames and Brevity

Dear Jordan,

The tour guide and art gallery analogy worked for your group? Terrific! I thought it might resonate with you, knowing your degree is in fine arts. It's encouraging when you try something and it makes sense. There are, of course, other ways to think about such a practice. One congregation I know calls them "in-between words." A fine worship leader I know calls them the mortar between the basic building blocks of a service.[3] A seminary teacher I heard describes them as tendons that connect the bones.

Whatever we call them (though I'll likely stick with the frame image), one of the biggest dangers when using them is to get verbose. We preacher and worship leader types love words and love explaining things. We grow comfortable hearing ourselves speak. So the temptation is to overexplain, to indulge our love for historical facts or our interest in theology. But the vision here is simply to introduce various elements of the service as it goes along, for first time attendees and regular attendees, for children and adults.

Let me put it another way: a winsome one- or two-sentence orientation is usually far better than a paragraph of the most theologically erudite excursus. There are exceptions, of course, but it's a good pattern for beginning. Work hard to make it jargon-free. (We used to charge novice worship leaders a dollar for every word of Christian jargon they used. It worked for a while—maybe because we spent the money on chai lattes for our team. But

2. Thanks to Tim Blackmon, who first suggested and articulated the wayfinding metaphor.

3. I first heard this image from Karl Digerness of City Church San Francisco.

it felt awkward over time. Some experienced it as something closer to shame than the kind of friendly accountability we intended. Still, everyone got the point.) Imagine using a frame like this:

> When we confess our sins, we are not groveling in guilt, but dealing with it. If you deny your sins you will never get free from them. So in the next few moments, let's admit the ways we've participated in the brokenness of the world and receive God's forgiveness.

I have a friend who begins every worship service with a kind of orientation, a brief conversation that describes the meaning of worship. Over time, he says, it helps newcomers know how to participate well in worship.[4]

I'd suggest you address people directly, as skeptics and novices and self-assured spiritual people from a variety of backgrounds. Assume they are in the room even if they are not when you first begin the practice. One of our pastors often frames passing the peace like this:

> This may seem a strange and awkward practice. But we do this because God in Christ extends his peace to us, so we in turn extend it to one another. This may feel awkward, but that's okay. Let's be awkward together and pass the peace of Christ.[5]

If you do run this by your group, I'd be fascinated to know what they think.

Much grace, (see how pithy my letter's sign-off is?!)
Kevin

On Worshiping as Part of the Holy Catholic Church (All Saints' Day)

Dear Jordan,

Someone in your group found a book by the theologian Alexander Schmemann? At a garage sale? Between a biography about baseball legend Hank Aaron and several classic books by Dr. Seuss? What are the odds? My wife is a fine mathematician, but even she might not be able to calculate those odds! Something similar happened to a friend of mine. He had recently retired, moving from California to the Midwest. In his new hometown he went garage-saleing only to have his wife pull up a yellow book and ask,

---

4. Inspired by Tim Keller's "Evangelistic Worship" paper.
5. Thanks to Sam Gutierrez for the first version of this frame.

"Isn't this a friend of yours?" She was holding a copy of *my* book—a valued commodity, apparently, priced at a quarter.

Still, that's terrific. A godsend! Schmemann is a wonderful theologian whose work you can find on many pastors' bookshelves and Kindles. And it's no wonder, captured by the book jacket's summary, that she bought it and keeps reading!

I love reading Schmemann and find him an inspiring and clarifying voice on worship and worldview. He was a much-published and much-appreciated Russian Orthodox priest who was popular in the 1960s. But I didn't hear about Schmemann until I taught a graduate school course on worship. If you had asked me about recommending him, I might have assumed he would be an acquired taste, for worship nerds only. That's why I'm so taken that your eclectic group has growing enthusiasm for his ideas. If you want to read something he wrote, you can't do better than his classic *For the Life of the World*. It's read and loved by people and groups as diverse as yours.

In fact, your group's enthusiasm has me thinking again about the value of frames that clearly show how our worship treasure is part of the broader holy catholic church (in honor of Schmemann, we might add the Orthodox Church). We've talked about this in planning meetings with our congregation. What if once in a while we help our attendees clearly see how our worship practice is part of the church of all times and places? For instance, what if we created a worship frame quoting Schmemann himself? Consider:

> Alexander Schmemann, a fascinating Russian Orthodox priest and teacher of worship, once said, "Each week in the liturgy the church 'enacts itself.'" We become our true selves in the liturgy. Part of our becoming our true selves happens in the practice of confession and assurance. This act forms us into braver, more honest people. We more deeply know our true selves and we more deeply know the God who forgives and makes new.
>
> In honesty there is freedom. So confession becomes the work of the church at worship. In this ancient practice, we ask for and receive forgiveness. No wonder this rhythm of confession and acceptance has been part of Christian worship services for all time.

Or think about another frame for confession formed by the story of a more well-known Christian personality, Augustine of Hippo:

> The rhetorical skill of a bishop drew him to faith. An expert orator himself, he became an accomplished preacher, able to reach his most learned and impious listeners. Once in the faith, he

became a highly regarded church leader, a skillful theologian, and a long-standing bishop. In his forties, he wrote a book that many consider the world's first autobiography.

Still, after all his sermons and service, he felt hopelessly contaminated. He passed his final days in a plain, barely furnished room. As thugs besieged the gates of his beloved city, he prayed in unadorned solitude, deluged by the memories of sins he committed. Regrets flooded his mind. Feeling polluted, he pored over his failed attempts at love and peace. Grace, not sin, was his main word. Yet in his final days he felt desperate for a glimpse of such comfort. So, at his request, large-lettered copies of four psalms were affixed to the walls of his cell. Four psalms. And nothing else. Seeing the words from his bed, he prayed them again and again, lamenting his sins as a bishop. A proven wordsmith and eloquent spokesman, he could think of no better way to express his heart's cry than to join those who recite Psalm 130. Let's use that as our confession this morning, "Out of the depths I cry . . ."[6]

If you are able, what about putting an image of the person you're referring to on the printed page or projected screen?

While naming specific people who belong to the global church might not work in every congregation, I wonder if the general idea—telling stories of the faith in the spirit of Hebrews—can work in most settings. Imagine a church introducing confession or passing the peace with a frame rehearsing the story of Martin Luther King Jr., or one that introduces the offering by telling about Dorothy Day, or frames a song by telling the story of an author like Charles Wesley or Wallace Willis?

Such frames might by nature be thick, and when used would mean the rest of the frames used in that service would need to be especially lean. But tell me what you think of this:

> John was born into a carefree life of privilege. Often, he acted the playboy, bedding women and writing brilliant ditties inspired by his favorites. He penned such gems as "A Defense of Woman's Inconstancy" and "Why Do Women Delight in Feathers?" (His answer was that women were "flighty.")
>
> An early portrait features him as a wealthy, young gentleman of means and social standing. His intricate lace collar,

---

6. Adapted from my book *150: Finding Your Story in the Psalms*. There I note, "The Augustine legacy still casts a long shadow in church teaching and practice. Soon after his death, the church gathered the psalms of his last days, and a few others, into a collection called the seven penitential psalms" (168). The others are 6, 32, 38, 51, 102, and 143.

the gold-feathered sleeve, and his folded arms show haughty confidence.[7]

A series of tragedies and missteps changed him. His family's Catholic origins fell out of vogue with the changing British monarchy. Events beyond his control thwarted his enduring desire to secure a position in the royal court. He fell madly in love with a noblewoman far above his social standing, but he secretly wed her anyway, violating her father's wishes and those of the royals.

His miscalculation, in the highly stationed life of sixteenth-century England, led him to prison and then a decade of poverty.

Desperate for a livelihood, a friend urged him to consider the priesthood. But John Donne thought it best to avoid such a calling, believing what he called "certain irregularities" from his past disqualified him.[8] Don't we all have "certain irregularities" in our lives that disqualify us from ministry or faith or forgiveness? Don't we understand the "constant guilt" he felt for not being a good enough husband or father or person? Let's confess our sins using the words of John Donne:

> Batter my heart, three-person'd God, for you
> As yet but knock, breathe, shine, and seek to mend;
> That I may rise and stand, o'erthrow me, and bend
> Your force to break, blow, burn, and make me new.
> I, like an usurp'd town to another due,
> Labor to admit you, but oh, to no end;
> Reason, your viceroy in me, me should defend,
> But is captiv'd, and proves weak or untrue.
>
> Yet dearly I love you, and would be lov'd fain,
> But am betroth'd unto your enemy;
> Divorce me, untie or break that knot again,
> Take me to you, imprison me, for I,
> Except you enthrall me, never shall be free,
> Nor ever chaste, except you ravish me.[9]

Or consider a similar introduction that ends with this poem as an alternative:

> Forgive me, O Lord,
> O Lord, forgive me my sins,
> the sins of my youth,
> and my present sins,

7. Stubbs, *John Donne*, 63.
8. Stubbs, *John Donne*, 232.
9. Stubbs, *John Donne*, 330.

the sin that my parents cast upon me,
original sin,
and the sins that I cast upon my children,
in an ill example;
actual sins,
sins which are manifest to all the world,
and sins which I have so labored to hide from the world,
as that now they are hid from mine own conscience,
and mine own memory.

Forgive me my crying sins,
and my whispering sins,
sins of uncharitable hate,
and sins of unchaste love,
sins against thee and against thy power, O almighty Father,
against thy wisdom, O glorious Son,
against thy goodness, O blessed Spirit of God;
and sins against him and him,
against superiors and equals,
and inferiors;
and sins against me and me,
against mine own soul,
and against my body,
which I have loved better than my soul.

Forgive me, O Lord,
O Lord, in the merits of thy Christ and my Jesus,
thine anointed,
and my savior.

Forgive me my sins,
all my sins,
and I will put Christ to no more cost,
nor thee to more trouble,
for any reprobation or malediction that lay upon me,
otherwise than as a sinner.

Amen.

Not every congregation will warm to John Donne's poetry as an occasional confession. But some will. My friend Neal says the frames for worship we've been talking about "introduce readers to the depth of Christian riches every week." I think he's right. And it made me glad to hear it. But of course, I'm curious what you and your team think.

In the great company of Jesus' followers,
Kevin

November

On Skeptics (Real and Imagined) Inside and Outside Church

Dear Jordan,

How can we be *sure* there are skeptics in your congregation?

My simplest and perhaps visceral reaction is this: because there is a skeptic in each of us. We are all like the man who came to Jesus desperate for his daughter's healing and said, "I do believe; help me overcome my unbelief!"[1] Your question also makes me think of the title of a sermon by the American theologian H. Richard Niebuhr: "Doubting Believers and Believing Doubters."[2] Doesn't that title sum us up?

After three decades of pastoral ministry, I'm convinced there are skeptics in *every* congregation. Is that elder with unending and exorbitant demands really posturing to cover up his disbelief? Is that young adult who grew up in the church really the model of faith she seems to be, or is she simply working up the courage to step outside everyone's expectations? And that vocalist just diagnosed with cancer—might he really be thinking in the recesses of his heart, "Do I *really* believe this?" And that's just the regular attendees! Most weeks even the most ensconced congregation has a visitor or two: someone's niece or a visiting tourist, perhaps an attendee's husband or granddaughter coming simply to get back in someone's good graces.

We have found over the years that simply naming the reality of doubt is helpful. And the presence of skeptics or spiritual novices only accents the need to be brief. Welcome everyone, and talk to them briefly and directly: "Some of you don't believe this; others of you aren't sure if you do . . ."

Often in our congregation the person preaching will offer a prayer before the sermon, historically called the Prayer of Enlightenment, that names the variety of faith experiences in the room:

1. Mark 9:24, NIV.
2. Niebuhr, "Doubting Believers and Believing Doubters."

Father, here we are, some of us feeling doubt, others slightly embarrassed that we're desperate enough to be in church, still others wobbly in what for so long felt like solid faith and a sure bet, and all of us asking now that you will speak to us your good news. Would you whisper your grace to us?

As you're hearing, worship frames not only explain each element, but can also express skepticism and disbelief. We work to voice objections to belief, to empathize with the difficulty of faith even as we invite people inside. Imagine acknowledging doubts even at an Easter service, often a time people feel as if they are *supposed* to believe. What might happen in your congregation if you frame an Easter prayer like this:

> Jesus' resurrection that first Easter was a complete surprise. For three years Jesus taught his disciples about the kingdom of God. For three years they watched him heal lepers and give sight to the blind. For three years he told them he would "die and rise again." But then it happened. And in the words of the Gospel of Luke, "But they did not believe the women, because their words seemed to them like nonsense."[3] If you doubt this story, even on Easter morning, you have good company. *Apostolic* company. Let's pray together to the God of surprise.

We find people who doubt, and their Christian spouses or friends or colleagues who invited them to church are grateful for the hospitality for skeptics—especially when you articulate their position as fairly and accurately as possible. It's as if you knew they were going to be there. Or as if your own doubt helped you understand theirs.

I'm curious to get your reaction, and that of your team, to all this.

Kevin

On the Helpfulness of Questions in Church and Liturgy

Dear Jordan,

I'm glad when you raised the issues of doubt in church that your group was so wonderfully (alarmingly?) honest. It sounds as if when Shanice and James opened up, the rest of the group followed. It's a gift to have such camaraderie and honesty. It speaks to your authentic leadership and to the permission you're giving people on your team to truly be themselves. And I agree, as you state so clearly and wonderfully, that the demands of working

---

3. Luke 24:11, NIV.

with your multicultural and multigenerational team nourishes the honesty and grace you experience, allowing you to get beyond surface chit-chat to form community.

I wonder if your group might benefit from knowing how their own questions can enhance worship leading. Often worship elements sound like statements passed on doubt-free from generation to generation of Christians. Those leading worship make them appear neat and tidy, formal and formulated, as if they dropped directly from heaven. But in reality, many of the classic elements of a worship service are answers to questions. What if you and your team framed them as such? Suppose a worship leader introduces the Lord's Prayer in this way:

> One day, after years of following Jesus, his disciples gathered the courage to ask him something that had been bothering them: how should we pray? They were raised in religious homes and in a religious culture, but they didn't know how to pray. We wonder too, don't we? In a world like ours, how are we supposed to pray? In the next few moments let's pray the prayer Jesus gave his disciples in response to their questions.

Or imagine someone hearing the Apostles' Creed for the first time. It might seem doctrinaire, like theological exactitude formulated by academics in a musty, book-filled room. But in reality, it took the church 300 years to articulate this creed. Entire careers rose and fell by its formulation. People were exiled or disavowed for assenting to or for refusing its content. What if your team, knowing their own struggles and those of our New Testament friends, framed the creed like this:

> Maybe you came today unsure about Jesus and his identity. You're not alone. It took his early followers 300 years to formulate what they believed about him. Yes, 300! In the next moments, we are all invited to use their words as a confession. We invite you, maybe for the first time, to try them on, to recite this creed, maybe as an answer to your own questions.

If questions feel foreign in a worship service, consider the model of the psalms. They are the songbook of Jewish worship and early Christian worship. And what we find in them speaks to our inmost beliefs and doubts, but by inviting people to express their questions from *inside* the faith, not outside. Some people assume we need to get clarity on what we believe and how we will live before we can enter a church community. But as the psalms show, God invites us to enter his community and voice our tangle of emotions and hopes and anxieties. He invites us to voice them in covenantal speech. Consider Psalm 13. It begins with five questions. Five. As if one isn't enough. It's no accident the church has long encouraged (expected?) psalms to be a foundational part of every worship service.

Alas, I fear I may be preaching now. But come to think of it, honest doubts are a gift to the task of preaching as well. The best preachers I know are in touch with their own doubts and those of their neighbors.

Lord, we believe; help our unbelief.
Kevin

On Mission, the Global Church, and the Liturgical Year

Dear Jordan,

It sounds again as if the varied backgrounds and life experiences of your team—such a wonderful gift—are surfacing. Some team members are excited to begin exploring and living the wisdom of what's called the liturgical year, while others think the topic irrelevant, a relic of the past. The irony, of course, is that the purpose of this worship practice is to unite congregations with their fellow Christians within the global church.

I'm particularly taken by Zendaya's story. Thanks for passing it on. It's a gift that she's part of your group. It's no wonder that as a child growing up in South Africa in a congregation with strong Anglican roots, her church followed the calendar of the Christian year and used the lectionary. Neither is it a surprise she "didn't have any concept or understanding of it." Many graduate students in theology share such unfamiliarity. And since she came to a deeper understanding of faith in a more general evangelical context, while attending a Baptist school and a Presbyterian youth group, it's no wonder she, like others in your group, hasn't thought about the liturgical calendar in years.

Like you, and like most people in your group who find the idea unfamiliar or even bewildering, I didn't grow up with the Christian year either. It wasn't until I started attending seminary that I was introduced to it. Even then it seemed a pattern of worship favored by more formal—dare I say *stuffy*?—congregations. Congregations and church leaders passionate about mission tossed it aside. Not until I experienced it at a vibrant urban congregation awash in mission did I consider introducing it in our congregation. The liturgical calendar tells the story of Christian faith via a yearly cycle of integrated Bible texts. Many—perhaps most?—find it a clear, meaningful framework for a year-long pattern of worship. It frees congregations from the potential tyranny of the individual preferences of one or two local leaders. I hope your team and your friends inside and outside the church will find it a gift as well. In a frantic city environment like yours, a wise framework can connect people to a rhythm of life that helps keep them sane.

Jordan, you're a natural and captivating storyteller. Often the liturgy can feel formal or even stuffy. But what if you and others in your group frame the liturgical year as a way to enter, live, and experience God's *story*? I've used the following in our church. What if you send me something original, and we'll talk about both frames before Sunday?

> We live in a world of stories. CNN, Fox News, ESPN, Nickelodeon, and the Discovery Channel have this in common: they tell stories. And they expect the stories they tell to shape the ways we live and think and behave. Yes, they also dispense information, but even the information comes in the form of story.
>
> God majors in stories too. The Bible isn't mostly a list of commands or rules or prophecies, but a collection of stories. Each invites us to enter into God's story and let it be ours.
>
> Today we begin a new liturgical year. Wise Christians created this annual series of Bible readings as a way for spiritual novices and veterans to enter more deeply into the Bible's story. Christians from around the world use this guide to frame their worship, and we'll be joining them again this year. As we begin this yearly calendar again with the season of Advent, we invite you to hear the grace-filled story and make it your own.

Or how about the following?

> A friend first began interacting with the liturgical year through a smartphone app. He wanted to read from the Bible every day but felt unmotivated and apathetic. His sporadic daily Bible readings and randomly chosen passages weren't inspiring anymore. He felt like a baffled explorer wandering aimlessly through the Bible. Lost.
>
> Then, using his new app, he began to follow set readings. At first he didn't notice much effect. He would often pick and choose from among the set passages, deciding for himself what he engaged. But he kept at it. Flash forward to a year later: he finds himself craving (yes, *craving*) this time in his day. As he entered into these readings, these readings entered into him. He found himself hearing and living God's story of grace.
>
> Today, as a congregation and with Christians around the world, we begin an annual cycle of set Sunday readings. It may seem odd or unfamiliar at first, but it's a way for us to enter into God's big story—*the* story. Even if the liturgical year feels new,

we invite you to step into this grand story and see if it helps you make sense of yours.

All best,
Kevin

On Framing the Liturgical Year and Dancing South African Style

Dear Zendaya (and Jordan),

Jordan is right! You *are* a wonderful worship leader. I love your draft frame— so personal, so alive, so apropos. The video you sent is contagious! Let me confirm you're okay with us using a slightly edited transcript of your frame:

> In South Africa, where I grew up, dance is essential to culture. It's impossible to imagine life without dance. Children dance from the moment they can walk. We have many dances, but a famous one is the Gwara Gwara. It's a traditional dance inspired by weddings, battles and everyday rituals. In South Africa, it feels as if we leave the womb ready to dance, but the truth is all of us need to learn the steps, to practice the moves. At first any dance feels new, even awkward. We can see why tourists would rather hide in the shadows. But eventually you find you are no longer learning the steps; you are dancing, and then comes the day you don't have to think about it.
>
> The liturgical year is like that. It's a kind of spiritual choreography that shapes our lives. Our moves mirror God's. We perform movements that "reflect God's waiting, giving, telling, turning, dying, rising and pouring out."[4] In each season of the liturgical year, we rehearse certain practices and we learn specific graces.
>
> Today we invite you to enter the dance of grace and to step into this year, and eventually every year, as a spiritual dance.

How wonderful! And given so many of your compatriots moving into your neighborhood, I can only imagine what resonance this will have. What if we also invite your group to create their own version for someone to say who doesn't share your unique story? Here's my first draft; I'd love your feedback:

---

4. Gross, *Living the Christian Year*, 27–28.

Some people seem able to dance the moment they leave the womb. They have a kind of grace, a fluidity of movement, an élan. Each step is exquisite.

The truth is that all of us need to learn the steps, to practice the moves. At first any dance feels new, even awkward. We become self-conscious wallflowers, tempted to hide in the shadows, to stand still. But step onto the dance floor and even the most awkward of us will eventually find we are no longer learning the moves; we are actually *dancing*!

The liturgical year is a kind of annual spiritual choreography.[5] Throughout the year we learn moves that mirror God's grace. Our movements "reflect God's waiting, giving, telling, turning, dying, rising and pouring out."[6] In each season of the liturgical year (Advent, Epiphany, Lent, Eastertide, and Ordinary Time), we rehearse steps that teach us particular graces.

If all this sounds a bit made up, consider that the early church fathers described life in the Trinity as a *perichoresis*—a kind of eternal dance—that we are invited to join.

Today, as we begin the liturgical year, we invite you to enter the dance of grace.

I'd love to hear your suggestions or edits. And maybe sometime, as you suggest, Jordan will invite me to meet with your team and you can teach us all the Gwara Gwara.

Or maybe some of us should simply sit and enjoy others' dancing instead?

Your friend with two left feet,
Kevin

The Liturgical Year: Holidays and Holy Days

Dear Jordan,

I couldn't resist sending a quick response. Thanks for sending such a wonderful frame. The notion of "holy-days" or holidays is a simple introduction to sacred time and the liturgical calendar. Each fast and feast invites us more deeply into the divine mystery.

Sometimes I envy your growing up with a full calendar of feast and fasting days. As you know, one of my good friends is a Greek Orthodox priest. The Orthodox Church calendar provides an entire year of feast

5. Gross, *Living the Christian Year*, 27.
6. Gross, *Living the Christian Year*, 28.

days (and fast days too) to live, including the birthday of your favorite and namesake saint. All of us can live more fully in this calendar. Let's imagine together someone framing the idea like this:

> We all live with special days circled on our calendar. We remember birthdays and anniversaries—our own and of those we love. Here in the United States we celebrate New Year's and Valentine's days, Martin Luther King Jr. Day, Memorial Day, Independence Day, and Thanksgiving. Our friends in other countries celebrate Cinco de Mayo and May Day, Canada Day, and Boxing Day.
>
> Christians, of course, famously celebrate Christmas and Easter. But there's an entire calendar of holy days to celebrate: Epiphany and Good Friday, Pentecost and Trinity Sunday. Today, as we begin a new liturgical year, let's encourage each other to pay attention to each to learn its particular grace.

Couldn't we also imagine a fuller, longer version? And why not create a shorter version too, framed in an interrogatory mood? What if each of us both draft some and send them to each other?

The more holidays the better!
Kevin

December

On Framing and Advent

Dear Jordan,

So there's still debate on your team—and in your congregation—about whether or not to set your preaching and worship schedule according to the liturgical year. I understand your foot-dragging. Advent does get some unwelcome press, especially from those who don't understand it. During December, many church attendees want to hear "Joy to the World" and read favorite Bible stories about baby Jesus. But instead of singing a steady stream of well-loved carols, churches that follow the liturgical year seem to sabotage one of the most captivating biblical stories by trading thoughts of baby Jesus for alarming prophetic and apocalyptic passages about the second coming and final judgment. During the very season the wider culture seems to turn toward the church, even singing its songs in malls and city streets, the church seems out of sync, turning to passages that focus on harsh divides between sheep and goats. How does one frame Advent?

Here are a couple of frames we use in our congregation. Knowing your team is currently brainstorming custom frames for your neighborhood, I'd love to hear how you might adapt these, or to explore together how we might go in a very different direction:

> Today is the first week of Advent. Both ancient and modern Christians consider Advent a time of spiritual preparation for Christmas. Advent means "coming." Each week we will celebrate Jesus' coming as a baby in Bethlehem and think about his second coming as King of the cosmos.

Or consider this Advent frame that accents the longing each of us experience regularly, especially in the weeks before Christmas:

> We all wish the world were a better place. Some days that wish is wistful thinking, a good idea that feels vague and far away.

Other moments, when we're in deep pain or when someone we love is suffering terribly, our longing can feel overwhelming, an ache beyond what our words can express.

During the season of Advent, the four weeks before Christmas, we celebrate God's creation and anticipate his re-creation. We voice our longing for God's healing renewal. We long for the day God will reach into our world of disorder and bring lasting peace.

Here's a different variation, with a little help from the famous New York director Woody Allen:

Woody Allen is said to have quipped: The lion and the lamb shall lie down together (as the prophet Isaiah foretells), but the lamb won't get much sleep!

Allen (if indeed he said this) was being cheeky. But he has a point. For all the harmony Isaiah describes, it isn't enough simply to design a display window of former foes sitting side by side. There will have to be some wholesale changes inside and out.

At the center of the season of Advent is a picture of shalom—a vision of universal flourishing of righteousness and justice for all. The poor and the needy will be treated with respect; the strong will no longer abuse the weak.

Old enemies, in other words, will need to do more than shake hands for a photo op. They have to wish each other well with every fiber of their being and then live in ways that will make that flourishing happen. This is Advent, and we long for that day together.[1]

For an advent frame that is deeply personal, accenting Mary's waiting as the first follower of Jesus, what about this?

Mothers know about waiting. Waiting to get pregnant. Waiting to hear a heartbeat. Waiting for the baby to kick. Waiting for the baby to be born. Waiting for the baby to nurse. Waiting for the baby to be quiet, or to walk, or to talk, or to smile.

Advent too is a time of waiting. We invite each other, like Jesus' mother, Mary, and the church of all times and places, to wait for Jesus. With Mary we ponder the coming of Immanuel.

I'd love to hear more about how your team expands this starter list, especially the waiting of Mary, since Protestants don't often give her the

---

1. Thanks to Scott Hoezee and the Center for Excellence in Preaching for inspiring this frame.

regard she deserves, and maybe others give her a little too much. Given the nature of your team, you will likely have a provocative discussion together.

In the hope of shalom,
Kevin

On Designing Advent Frames Inspired by Our Heritages and Countries of Origin

Dear Jordan,

Thanks for passing on such a unique and beautiful Advent frame. It's genius on Mateo's part to use stories from his Mexican heritage to create a custom frame. It's stirring how global Christian traditions like *Las Posadas*—couples pretending to be Mary and Joseph looking for room at the inn—survive massive cultural change and help us see in such a personal way that we all belong to the global church.

Don't you have a team meeting this week? What if, inspired by Mateo's example, you ask each team member to write a frame for Advent (or another upcoming liturgical season) that connects to their personal story and heritage? My hunch is that everyone has a relatable story, and helping each other use their stories to create frames will be a wonderful gift.

One way to make worship frames resonate with a congregation's particular neighborhood and to find a congregation's unique worship voice is to design frames based on personal stories of attendees. Then, rather than frames being something borrowed or brought in from other congregations or books on worship, they become part of the Holy Spirit's unique work in a particular congregation. In Advent terms, we might think of it as working out God's incarnation in fresh ways.

One of our worship leaders, also of Mexican upbringing, was inspired by Mateo to create her own frame based on her country of origin. Before she uses it, we'd value Mateo's permission and his feedback:

> I grew up in Oaxaca, Mexico. Though it's been a long while since I lived there, many of the dates on my inner calendar flow from my childhood: Our Lady of Guadalupe Day (December 12), El Día de los Tres Reyes Magos (Three Kings Day), Christmas Eve (Nochebuena). In Mexico, people often keep their holiday decorations up well past Christmas, all the way to February 2 (Feast of the Presentation).
>
> But the days dearest to my heart were the last nine days of Advent. Local couples acting out the story of Joseph and

Mary would go door-to-door in a custom known as Las Posadas (meaning "the inns").

They knocked on someone's front door and waited. There they stood. Outside. Wondering. Vulnerable. Like Joseph and Mary. Is there room for us?

Eventually we'd open the door. Then we'd sing, back and forth, the couple from the porch outside and the family or friends gathered inside.

That waiting, more than anything else, stirred childhood wonder. Of course, the star-shaped piñatas awaiting my cousins and me after the singing may have helped this memory linger in my imagination.

That waiting symbolizes the season of Advent. We are invited to wait. We wait for peace and harmony. We wait for the lion and the lamb to lie down together. We wait for doors to open. For the singing to begin. And for the King to come.

Pass on our deep gratitude to Mateo for sharing his story.

Vaya con Dios,
Kevin

On Advent Groaning

Dear Jordan,

Thanks for reaching out to Manuela and affirming her frame. As Mateo said in giving her permission to use his frame as an inspiration for her own, "Imitation is the sincerest form of flattery." Folks in our congregation were really helped, even moved, by Manuela's words.

To answer your question, I don't think you are off base. Giving people permission to groan, to grieve, and to lament is a deep part of the Advent season.[2] Your email made me want to write a worship frame for our service this week; it's my turn to lead a prayer in our congregation:

> It's Christmastime. Some of us love this season and its great food, familiar music, and presents. Christmas makes many of us alive with rich memories and good feelings. But others of us want to go into hiding. We feel the strong pull of temptation and obligation. We feel swallowed in debt. Some feel a fresh dose of grief for those we miss. We're discouraged by daily news feeds and holiday hoopla gone sour. I have a neighbor who went on vacation every Christmas to avoid it.

2. Gross, *Living the Christian Year*, 44.

For generations, wise Christians have called the four weeks before Christmas Advent. In Advent, we groan together as a global church, for a better world, and a better version of ourselves. Together, let's pray an Advent prayer of waiting.

Maybe, depending on how long this week's preacher thinks the sermon will be, I'll use a very simple version or thinner frame for the above. What do you think of this?

Advent is a time of longing. We long for a better world. We long for a better neighborhood. We long for better selves. Let's join the church of all times and places and pray a prayer of Advent longing.

I'm so glad to be learning from each other!
Kevin

On the Twelve Days of Christmas and Christmas Carols

Dear Jordan,

You asked for a sample Christmas frame we use at our church. I'm happy to share one. A few years ago, one of our worship leaders said a version of this. His comments reflect his pastoral presence and energy—full of childlike wonder and joy. Overflowing with delight, he looked our congregation straight in the eye and said with a face and voice full of good cheer:

When Christians celebrate the birth of Jesus, we don't just celebrate for an evening or for a day, but for twelve! We invite you, in the spirit of Christians past and present, to celebrate this season for twelve full days, to eat and drink and be merry for each of them. A miracle has happened. God has become human. And we want to feast!

For those in our church not sure about following the liturgical year, this was a clear reason to be converted. Here's another frame we use to introduce our offering (the beginning might sound familiar):

On the first day of Christmas my true love gave to me
a partridge in a pear tree.
On the second day of Christmas my true love gave to me
two turtle doves . . .
We give gifts at Christmas and before. We distribute clothing to those experiencing homelessness; we offer gifts to children

of prisoners; we send gifts (thank you, Amazon) to friends and
family far away.

The historic church didn't end their gift-giving on Christmas Day. Christmas was a twelve-day season in which they celebrated God's gift of Jesus by giving gifts themselves. We invite
you to continue your generosity all through the season.

Over the years we've tried a frame or two centered on the *other* major figure of the Christmas season, one who seems almost omnipresent in
December:

The Dutch call him Sinterklaas; the British, Father Christmas;
the Germans, Kris Kringle. Brazilians know him as Papai Noel
who brings gifts from the *South* Pole.

Saint Nicholas was born in Myra, in what is now the country
of Turkey. He lived in the late 200s and early 300s and became a
bishop. His great generosity, especially to children in need, was
legendary. One tale tells of a merchant who lost everything and
so had no dowry for his daughters. But each time the need came
they found a sack of gold thrown over the wall of the house and
filling a stocking that was hung to dry. Whatever we call him,
this saint points to God, the great Christmas giver, and encourages us to be givers as well.

Maybe you can talk about Santa in your church; maybe not. For some
households, talking about Santa has profound spiritual and family implications. But hopefully we can all agree that generosity is a Christian practice
we want to accent during this season.

At our worship team's Christmas party, we celebrated with many of the
usual Christmas traditions: we exchanged gifts, drank eggnog, and ate too
many desserts. At one point our superb lead musician suggested we all use
a favorite Christmas carol to write a worship frame. Earlier that day he felt a
bit uncertain about his own idea and asked for my reaction. He didn't want
a Christmas party to feel like *work*. But it was sheer delight. Much-loved
and repeated carols were new all over again. In hearing each other's frames
we reveled in each other's stories, in our story together, and in the amazing
truth of the babe of Bethlehem. Everyone knows I love the psalms, but they
we still a bit surprised by my choice:

Isaac was always weak and sickly, malnourished and barely five
feet tall. Though weak in body, he was strong in mind and spirit
and poetry. After one Sunday morning service, Isaac, then fifteen, complained about the awful music. A deacon challenged,

"Give us something better." Isaac's answer was ready for the evening service.

He composed many songs we still sing, such as "When I Survey the Wondrous Cross" and "O God Our Help in Ages Past." But his most famous may be his least likely. Sickly all his life, spurned by a woman he hoped to marry, physically awkward with a disproportionately large head, and plagued by inner mental torment, he borrowed words from Psalm 98 to create one of the most beloved and joyful hymns ever. It helps us revel in what Jesus' birth means to all of us. We call it "Joy to the World."

No, that frame didn't write itself spontaneously at our party. I don't store so much biographical information on Isaac Watts in my memory. I could write that frame because I had just given a Christmas-themed lecture on him to donors to a local Christian college. But I share it because it represents how personal and touching each frame was that evening. We sang carol after carol, each made new by the person and story that introduced them. One especially poignant frame came from one of our interns. She said,

> When I was a child I seldom slept through the night.
> Nightmares woke me up and kept me awake.
> You can only imagine how exhausting this was for my parents.
> They didn't know what to do. Or say.
> So my dad would sing. And one of his favorites—and mine too—was "Away in a Manger." Even during the suffocatingly hot days of August or the crisp days of autumn, softly and gently he would sing, "Away in a manger, no crib for a bed . . ."
> Sometimes I think Jesus is real to me today because of that song.

When she finished, we were all in tears. To think of a heavenly Father singing God's love via an earthly father. Some experts say millennial believers don't find classic worship songs speaking to their soul. This one clearly does.

Merrily yours, for twelve days and beyond,
Kevin

On Christmas Eve, the Incarnation, and Christmas Mystery

Dear Jordan,

Your neighbor is absolutely right. Christmas Eve *is* the number one time people reengage the church. Already back in the fifth century, following the lead of a congregation in Jerusalem, churches began holding a midnight Mass on Christmas Eve. Author and playwright T. S. Eliot called Christmas "the still point of the turning world . . . where past and future are gathered."[3] It's no wonder people from all spiritual backgrounds love this time of year.

During a season overstuffed with cliché, high-octane sentiment, and sugar overdoses, how do we frame what people think they already know? What about naming this mystery, accenting what we *don't* know?

> Today we celebrate Christmas, the Feast of the Incarnation. This reality is beyond belief and understanding: that almighty God became one of us. In this mystery, we can't fathom Jesus is fully human, but no less God. It took hundreds of years and many church councils to try to make sense of this. But we might simply ask ourselves what the incarnation might mean for us personally. How might we open our hearts to the presence of Jesus, to the God who comes to us as a baby?

That could frame a carol, or an offering, or a prayer. You also asked if we have any brief frames for the season of Christmas. Here's one:

> Everyone is singing our song. Listen, and you'll hear Christmas carols everywhere—in malls and elevators and Costco and at the gas pump. Carols are simply songs that tell stories, and especially now, they are songs that tell the story of Christmas. Let's listen.

Or another:

> It's no accident that lights are everywhere at Christmas. Martin Luther first came up with the idea of putting lights on a tree brought inside, what he called a Yuletide tree. In a world that has too much darkness today, we celebrate Jesus as the light of world.

You might also imagine the core of *play* each liturgical season has. Even times of fasting, such as Lent, are designed to highlight the joy of the

---

3. Gross, *Living the Christian Year*, 69.

gospel. So why not revel in the joy inherent to the twelve days of Christmas? Consider this:

> Christmas is far from over. The church has long held that one day is just not enough to celebrate the good news of Christ's birth. We need twelve days! In the small town in Sussex, England, where I was born, we celebrated all twelve days of Christmas. We received gifts not just on one day, but on twelve! Consider that as we sing this carol together.

What do you think?

Happy Christmas,
Kevin

January

On Epiphany Frames for Worship and Preaching

Dear Jordan,

After surveying your team, it seems as if no one you know has heard of Epiphany? I'm not surprised. Many churches celebrate Advent; there's something inside us that wants to prepare for Christmas. Some people are familiar with Lent; the legacy of fasting and fish on Fridays still lingers in certain neighborhoods and pockets of culture. But Epiphany? Not so much.

Here are some ways we've tried to introduce it. I'm curious to hear whether you think they'll work in your setting. First:

> In the season of Epiphany, we celebrate and remember Jesus as
> *the* light. We explore what he does and what he says. With the
> Magi who followed the star, we seek Jesus, the light of the world.

It's simple, I know, but we've found a frame like that can help people understand and fully engage in a song, a Bible reading, or a call to confession. We've discovered that this season of the church year needs reinforcement. It's often new and unfamiliar. Last year during Epiphany, each person on our preaching team used a simple Epiphany frame to begin their sermon. We found that simple repetition both connected the weekly worship to preaching and reinforced the season and stories of Epiphany. Here's a poignant and pithy frame inspired by the wonderful storytelling preacher Fred Craddock. Its simplicity may be just what a particular service or season needs. Imagine saying this as an introduction or conclusion to each sermon during Epiphany:

> During Epiphany, the whisper in Bethlehem becomes a shout
> heard around the world.

Or imagine following that with an Epiphany text, or with praying.

Here's another frame that uses a description of the season. It leans in the direction of informing rather than framing, but maybe it's worth a try, or maybe it's something you could readily adapt:

> For generations, followers of Jesus after celebrating Christmas have thought about Jesus' life. It's a season we call Epiphany. It starts with two events: the Magi visiting baby Jesus, representing the entire world coming to Jesus for light, and Jesus' baptism, when he hears his Father say, "This is my Son, whom I love with him I am well pleased."[1]

Or maybe you want to directly emphasize the person and work of Jesus the way Epiphany accents his miracles and message:

> We all need a miracle. For some, the need is modest. We hope a certain someone will say yes when we ask them on a date. We hope our boss will give us a raise. We hope our toddler twins let us sleep through the night. For others, the miracle we need is a lot bigger. We hope the cancer treatments work. We pray our parents won't get divorced. We hope we find a job so the landlord won't take away our apartment. Or we hope our city's streets will be safe.
>
> During the season of Epiphany we rehearse the life and ministry of Jesus. We see again, or for the first time, the One who heals lepers, gives sight to the blind, and turns water into wine. As we pray this morning, let's turn to him.

Again, I'd love to see what you and your team are working on, or what you might do to improve and customize any of these.

Much grace,
Kevin

On Epiphany House Blessings and Including Outsiders

Dear Jordan,

Your information is right. During the past several years, we've begun an Epiphany tradition of blessing homes. We are amazed at how enthusiastically the Northern Californians in our congregation took to this tradition started in the Middle Ages. At a person's request, we visit a home and pray through it, going room to room. As the visit ends we anoint people with oil and water, inviting them to remember their baptism. Sometimes, following

1. Matt 3:17, NIV.

an ancient practice, we sign the letters B, M, and G on the doorpost of the home, initials for the traditional names of the original Magi: Balthasar of Arabia, Melchior of Persia, and Gaspar of India. We also pray a litany friendly to all ages that accents how Epiphany shows the light of Jesus going to our lives, our homes, and all nations. The visits are delightful moments of grace and a valuable connection between worship and pastoral care.

One of our team members alerted us that this Epiphany house blessing tradition originated in China. I recently read a newspaper story affirming this account and suggesting the original Magi were from China.[2] The story is based on a third-century book recently uncovered in a Vatican library and translated only a few years ago. It describes the Magi as an ancient mystical sect from the land of Shir "at the shore of the Great Ocean." In other texts, Shir is associated with silk production, leading the translator to identify Shir as China and the Magi as Chinese.

There's so much life-giving tradition to celebrate during Epiphany. Many countries celebrate the day of Epiphany as a feast day. You might want to check with your group to learn if anyone experienced such a tradition growing up. Here's an example of how we translated one of these themes into a frame we used last year:

> We are in the season the church calls Epiphany. During Epiph-
> any, we celebrate and remember Jesus as the light. We reflect on
> his life and teaching and healing. His light begins with us, in our
> lives and homes, and then spreads throughout the world. Let's
> invite Jesus to be our light.

Or imagine a frame that sets up passing the peace:

> During the season of Epiphany, we celebrate Jesus coming as
> the light of the world, and we celebrate his light spreading to
> every neighborhood and nation. As a symbol of receiving and
> sharing that light, turn to someone near you and say, "The peace
> of Christ be with you."

Built into the season of Epiphany is an emphasis on mission. Jesus is the light of the world—the whole world. As we celebrate and remember God's story, we also celebrate and remember the way he creates a church with people from *every* nation. Based on your sparkling way with words and your own captivating faith story, you could make a template that people from any heritage could use to frame this season:

2. Healy, "Were the Three Wise Men from China?"

At first Christmas seems like a Jewish story. The Bible makes a big deal about Joseph and Mary being descendants of Israel's most valiant and godly leader, King David. We can assume the innkeeper and those shepherds who told about Jesus were also Jewish, living as they did in a small town like Bethlehem.

But then in come the Magi, and with them the whole world. *Our* people, whoever we are—Bulgarians and Bolivians, Chinese and Czechs, Filipinos and French, the Dutch and the Navajo are now all at the center of the story of Jesus. Whoever you are, wherever you've been, the story now includes you. Let's celebrate our belonging by . . .

I often imagine the Magi sashaying into Jerusalem with tattoos and tarot cards and a bumper sticker affixed to their camel saying, "First palm reading is free." Clearly their questions unnerved the paranoid King Herod, and they still unnerve political posers today. Their entrance must have been unforgettable. Their exit surely was. These consummate outsiders show that, in Jesus, anyone can become an eternal insider. That's quite an Epiphany story to describe, to celebrate, and to frame. In fact, what about something simple, like this?

Epiphany reminds us that in Jesus' kingdom there are no spiritual outsiders. Magi come from the East. Shepherds come from their fields. Disciples are chosen from various political backgrounds. Jesus' clear message is that his light can come to any of us.

I hope that helps you get started on your own custom frames.

With you, happy to belong,
Kevin

On the Benefit of Frames for Neighborhood Conversations Outside and Inside the Church

Dear Jordan,

Isn't that amazing? Just as your group is wrestling with its own inner doubts and how and when to express them in worship frames, you have a heart-to-heart conversation with your daughter's softball coach. I've heard many stories like his: someone who grew up in church, felt doubts as an emerging adult, and assumed they had no choice but to leave. On one hand, we can honor his honesty. He saw his leaving as a matter of integrity. But now, fifteen years, a marriage, and three children later, he finds himself wondering again.

I don't find it surprising that our discussion on worship frames helped you navigate your conversation together. That's partly why this practice can be so helpful. With you, I'm particularly grateful that your invitation to probe his questions from inside the church, rather than feeling duty-bound to solve his inner faith riddles alone, resonated with him. I'm grateful too that after our conversation this idea more deeply resonates with you.

Part of the beauty of living in the neighborhood where we lead worship (as you know, I've been in ours for twenty-eight years) is that over time we speak in our community's particular language or accent. We know the particular dis-eases and diseases of their heart. We intuit their mental reservations. To put it in the language of worship frames, engaging in ministry from inside a neighborhood enables us to optimally articulate objections to following Jesus as clearly as—or even more clearly than—most skeptics can themselves.

Over time, our conversations, including our questions *in* worship, form and prepare us for conversations *outside* a worship service. And conversations in the neighborhood, like those at your daughter's softball field, form and prepare us for participating in worship.

I find most people who aren't connected to a particular religious faith aren't at all sure what they believe. They often draw their beliefs from a smorgasbord of sources: their favorite media personality, a favorite aphorism from a grandparent, and/or maybe a song that tugs at their heart. Often they're embarrassed even to speak their questions aloud. They're like a novice sailor, greenhorn gym rat, or adolescent biologist: not only can they not speak the language of faith, but they can't even articulate their questions. And their embarrassment silences them.

Last week a couple visited our congregation who hadn't worshiped with us for seven or eight years. When I greeted them they said, "We had to come back. Our children are asking us questions we can't answer. So this is a good place to get answers, right?" Right.

Most of the time, I find, folks hide their questions, afraid they don't know enough even to talk about what they don't know. So again, articulating questions and acknowledging them in worship is a wonderful gift for every attendee.

I hope you have more earnest conversation with the coach. It would be great, as you said, to see him inside a worship service. I can see how his attendance might energize your team for our worship frame project and perhaps inspire a frame:

We live in a world of experts. Mechanics need expertise to fix our cars. Doctors need expertise to prescribe medicine or perform surgery. But is that also true in worship? Is faith only for experts? Or is there room for novices? Epiphany reminds us that faith doesn't require expertise. In fact, such a false expectation makes faith fake. Faith doesn't require expertise—only humility in taking the next step toward the light.

Maybe you can send me a frame you're working on that involves your questions, or those of your neighbors?

With hope and curiosity,
Kevin

On the Benefit of Worship Frames for Longtime Attendees

Dear Jordan,

I'm still reveling in your conversation with your softball-coaching friend. And now to hear that another member of your team had a similar experience with her favorite barista? What delight! Sometimes opportunities simply appear. But it's a wonderful gift to have multiple team members experience firsthand how the *work* of worship—which is, as you know, what *liturgy* literally means—connects so clearly to the work of loving our neighbors.

Yesterday I received an email from one of my seminary students. He grew up in the church. He loves his neighborhood and its dazzling variety of people. His real passion, though, is teaching his community's adolescents. He serves as an AmeriCorps volunteer working with at-risk kids, and now he's training for ministry. He's bright, articulate, thoughtful, and eager to learn. You'd like him. A lot.

As part of our class on worship, we are talking about frames for worship—I'm sure you're not surprised. Though he's a lifelong church attendee, he was stunned to know that he'd participated in these worship elements, these treasures of the church, without any idea of their significance. His sorrow could become a frame:

> For years, I was completely unaware of the significance of my church's liturgy because it had never been explained to me. I wonder how many other worshipers are experiencing beautifully composed liturgies with no idea of the profound meaning being expressed.

How should a worship leader walk people through the liturgy in a way that highlights the purpose behind the practice? Should this be done during the service or as part of a class?

If it is the church who enacts the liturgy, how can a worship leader best prepare the church to understand the liturgy's meaning and engage it well?[3]

I'm taken by his plea. He's so earnest, and so heartsick. How could he grow up in a church, spending more than two decades in it, and not know the purpose of worship? It wasn't that he was merely going through motions. Rather, he didn't know the purpose or meaning of the motions. He was engaged—he prayed and sang and listened to sermons. It's just that his faith would have been deepened by knowing why the church was acting out those *particular* motions (or, to return to Zendaya's email, those particular dance steps).

He loves our undertaking and the notion that worship frames enable spiritual novices and skeptics to understand and more fully experience each worship element as a kind of life-giving treasure. But in his email I hear an entreaty for formation—his own, and that of people like him.

The good news is that these aren't mutually exclusive or competing sensibilities. A worship frame benefits skeptics, novices, returning softball coaches, long-time attendees—even people who lead worship.

What if we return to our image of a guide? If we spend enough time in a new art gallery, a zoo's panda exhibit, a hospital's operating room, or an auto mechanic's garage, we can begin to learn some vocabulary and gain some understanding on our own. But how much more readily will we learn and absorb and value if we are oriented and taught by a veteran, a contagiously enthusiastic guide (or wayfinder)! Again, I'm not talking about the kind of know-it-all who more than anything wants to show off his knowledge or wit, but rather the sort of guide who truly delights in the treasures before us.

Growing up, my blue-collar family's tastes ran more in the direction of outboard motors and fishing reels than to Pablo Picasso and Jackson Pollock. A few years ago, my wife and I entered a gallery that featured Picasso and Pollock and very provocative—and to us most puzzling—"floor art." For an hour, we wandered aimlessly, like clueless tourists who can't speak the local language. Left on our own we could have spent hundreds of hours without deepening our understanding of what we saw, heard, or (in some cases) walked upon. But then we signed up for a docent-led tour. In the hands of our capable tour guide, a volunteer art enthusiast, we learned more

---

3. Thanks to Josiah Gorter for permission to share his reflections from a Spring 2017 class at Western Theological Seminary.

in an hour than we could have by months of wandering around by ourselves, guessing at meaning. What's more, her contagious love for the art seeped into us. It's not that I'm now ready to purchase art to lie on my living room floor. But in some ways, I've taken the idea inside. I'm open to it. In a beginning way, I'm starting to "get it." And I'm curious to "get it" more.

Here's to worship frames,
Kevin

P.S. As Lent and Holy Week approach, I'd be especially interested to hear what your team is working on. Feel free to send the frames my way so we can talk about them together.

February

On Lent, Repenting, and Books That Help Us Frame

Dear Jordan,

Yes. Exactly. As you say, Lent is in many ways an extended focus on our need for confession, a time to meditate on Jesus' suffering. Given that, what about a simple frame like this, possibly to introduce a call to confession or a prayer?

> The word *repentance* can bring to mind experiences of shame, or ridicule, or the minor-key songs of a revival-meeting altar call. But healthy repentance is simply a way to be honest. The season of Lent reminds us that in a world of dodging and blame, healthy people look clearly in the mirror and admit the truth about themselves.

Or imagine beginning a worship service with a frame like this, making Lent a natural rhythm, framing confession as a constant, daily rhythm of the Christian life, like breathing out and breathing in:

> In our better moments, we want to cultivate habits that help us see the truth about who we are. But our ongoing brokenness tempts us to fog up any mirror that shows our sin. We quickly and instinctively move to justify our self or minimize our mistakes. So we need God—to save us, to love us, and to make us known. Lent teaches us to trust this mercy, to receive his forgiveness.

Here's another for confession:

> During the season of Lent, we remember that we do not gather as "pretty good people." It's not just other people—people "out there"—who mess up God's good creation. *We* do. We contribute to our own failures: we cheat, we slander, we posture to gain

applause. Thankfully, Lent also reminds us that despite ourselves, we are new people because of Jesus. He marks us with his grace. We are no longer defined by our failures and successes. We are free.

My friend Neal Plantinga puts it this way (like a beautifully simple frame) in his masterful book *Not the Way It's Supposed to Be: A Breviary of Sin*:

> Recalling and confessing our sin is like taking out the garbage: once is not enough.[1]

If you like that (I sure do!), what about another pithy Lenten frame inspired by Neal?

> Human society, as C. S. Lewis puts it, is a group in which "minimum decency passes for heroic virtue and utter corruption for pardonable imperfection."[2] But the truth teaches us we need saving from our sin.

And one more. Imagine quoting him directly, saying something like this:

> In his book *Not the Way It's Supposed to Be*, author Neal Plantinga writes, "The image of pollution suggests bringing together what ought to be kept apart. To pollute soil, air, or water is to blend into them foreign materials—machine oil, for example—so that these natural resources no longer nourish or delight very well. Similarly, the introduction of a third lover into a marriage or an idol into the natural human relation with God adds a foreign agent to them; it corrupts these entities by addition."[3] In the next few moments we are going to look straight at pollution, call it evil, and receive grace from the one who can truly scrub clean all of creation.

As you can see from these quotes, the writing of a superb author can be a gold mine of framing inspiration.

With you, longing for shalom,
Kevin

---

1. Plantinga, *Not the Way It's Supposed to Be*, x.
2. Plantinga, *Not the Way It's Supposed to Be*, 182.
3. Plantinga, *Not the Way It's Supposed to Be*, 45.

On Fasting, Baptism, and Family as Images for Lenten Frames

Dear Jordan,

That's a wonderful idea overflowing with the wisdom of believers who have gone before us. You're so right, and wise, to connect or frame the forty days of Lent as part of ongoing baptismal preparation practices. I love that you're learning how the season of Lent began as a preparation for new believers to be baptized. As a teacher, it's good to know that ministerial education is being so personally and practically helpful.

So yes, I think you're right (and not just because I've taught in a seminary setting) that helping worshipers to understand how Lent functioned in the early church will invite people into living the story and taking in the teaching of the faith. What about a frame that accents the connection of baptism and Lent?

> Enough. A thousand voices tell us who we should be and what we should do. We must be clever, or fit, or beautiful (in a way that matches the person in the magazine), or smart. When we are not "enough," we hear voices of condemnation.
>
> Lent is a good time to hear again the voice of God. Not the voice we imagine from God—the curmudgeonly movie critic who holds up our failing ratings for everyone to see—but the God who goes to the cross and voices, "It is finished." God is our "enough."

Or we might introduce Lent with a family motif:

> We assume we need to prove ourselves to God as we do with everyone else. Maybe we picture God impatiently tapping his toes or waiting for an excuse to walk out on us. But the gospel truth is that God is the kind of parent who is waiting to reach out to us in love. We act like orphans, afraid we are alone. But God waits with arms open to grace.

What image might you use? You've hinted at your childhood "fish on Fridays" experience. What about something personal that invites people to rethink their connection with God? If fasting rules emphasize "oughts" and obligations, presenting God as a cold and distant arbiter of justice, maybe you could reframe fasting as something that accents joy?

I look forward to what you create!

All best,
Kevin

On Lent, and Saints Behaving Badly

Dear Jordan,

Thanks for passing on the heartfelt conversation with your flatmates. As you told them: They are right. The church has scoundrels; some days it seems full of them. This is another place where we see the intersection between informal conversations and those in the context of worship.

What do you think about simply acknowledging this reality, but not only in meal settings like you described? I too have been in situations where the alcohol present seemed to "enhance the honesty," as you put it. It's as if they wanted to tell you something for some time, but needed the right occasion. And Wednesday evening it was.

More than a few years ago, a local Borders bookstore closed. A confirmed bookaholic, I couldn't resist their clearance sale. One title from Thomas Craughwell was irresistible: *Saints Behaving Badly*. Its subtitle was more enticing still: *The Cutthroats, Crooks, Trollops, Con Men, and Devil-Worshippers Who Became Saints*.

On the back cover, journalist Raymond Arroyo beckoned, "Here are all your favorite intercessors with their venal, cranky, obnoxious, murderous tendencies intact. . . . If these folks can make the cut, maybe there's hope for the rest of us."[4]

The inside flap tantalized: "From thieves and extortionists to mass murderers and warmongers, up-close and embarrassingly personal snapshots of those sanctified people with the most unsaintly pasts in the history of Christianity."[5]

Later it sounded like a brag, calling itself "the first book to lay bare the less than saintly behavior of thirty-two venerated holy men and women, [presenting] the scandalous, spicy, and sleazy detours they took on the road to sainthood."[6]

Could you imagine making this into a worship frame? If I were doing it in our church, I might tell the story and, yes, make a Lenten confession of my bookaholic ways. But I think you could use it too. One personal approach might be to talk about the tainted history of the church in your country of origin.

This frame might get a bit long. But let's try something together. What if we introduce a Lenten confession inspired by Craughwell's book?

---

4. Craughwell, *Saints Behaving Badly*, cover material.
5. Craughwell, *Saints Behaving Badly*, cover material.
6. Craughwell, *Saints Behaving Badly*, cover material.

We imagine saints as godly, saintly, pristine, and holy. But many had a checkered past. Have you heard of Saint Olga, who unleashed a bloodbath on her husband's assassins?

What about Pelagia, a fifth-century Phoenician actress of notoriously easy virtue who seduced countless men before her conversion led her to a convent?

Or Moses—not the famous bearer of the Ten Commandments, but the one who began life in the fourth century as an Egyptian slave, then took up a life of crime and violence, raiding villages and robbing or killing travelers? While running from the law, he hid in a monastery where the monks' hospitality so overwhelmed him that he joined them!

Or Saint Olaf, who began training as a Viking raider when he was just twelve years old, learning to plunder and kill with a clear conscience until he took up with the Normans? He converted to Christianity and was baptized in 1013.

We could go on. And on. But instead, what if we follow their lead, turn from our sin, and pray to the God who forgives?

One of the saints in our congregation first introduced himself to me by saying, "Hey, Pastor, my name is Bob, and I'm a drunk." As you might have guessed, Bob was an active attender of Alcoholics Anonymous. A feisty ex-Marine, he had no patience for platitudes and false piety. I wept the day he visited my office and gave me his pin celebrating twenty-five years of sobriety. In the last days of his life he would shuffle into church and then forward for communion. Wouldn't it be fascinating to bring some of the directness of an AA meeting into a frame?

I look forward to your wisdom!
Kevin

On Pizza, Boy Scouts, and Wayfinding Worship Novices

Dear Jordan,

I love the story of your being in the middle of a pizza party for your son's Boy Scout troop when another parent abruptly asks, "So what's with those old prayers you say at your church anyway?"

It reminds me of the hundreds of times something similar has happened to me. I agree—it's disorienting. You're at an event, relaxing with your family, maybe keeping half an eye on the nearby screen tuned to your favorite team on ESPN. Your mind is focused on food, or your kids, or the conversation. But someone sees you and thinks "church!" So out blurts a question. It may feel a little unfair to have to field questions in such settings, but welcome to the club. The same thing happens to doctors and dentists and real estate agents. One of my friends, a physician assistant, says her mentor in medicine told her it's an honor to be asked heartfelt questions, even at inopportune moments. It shows trust.

As we've been saying all along, in that moment—especially with other folks around the table overhearing your answer—the shorter the reply, the better. One advantage of the kinds of worship frames we've been talking about is that designing a frame prepares you in advance to give a short, thoughtful response to impromptu questions about worship. Okay, so *thoughtful* is not how you would describe your stammering answer at the pizza place. You made it sound as if it veered more in the direction of a dazed and disoriented "What?" Amazing, isn't it? All our articulate theology and well-designed words evaporate in the face of sudden reality. Take heart. You'll be ready next time. But by then the question will change!

Your fellow befuddled traveler,
Kevin

P.S. Here's a thought. What if you share your story at your next worship team meeting? It shows humility and vulnerability, for one thing (people don't mind remembering their worship leaders are human!). Your momentary loss for words only accents our conversation about framing and the way it equips us as worship leaders (and the entire church) to be ready to answer heartfelt, impromptu questions. What if you and your team shape three brief replies to the very subjects that confounded you on the spot: explaining Eucharist, baptism, and "those old prayers"?

On Borrowed Prayers and the Eclectic Company of Those Who Pray Psalms

Dear Jordan,

Okay, that wasn't fair. I only resonated with your dazed incoherence, but didn't give you any real direction for framing the psalms—what your friend described as "those old prayers." As with so many worship elements, when our church first began we didn't pray them. We thought we needed to set the psalms aside to be relevant, and to connect with (or at least not to confuse) people like your questioning pizza-party friend. Psalms felt befuddling. They feature archaic images and centuries-away situations. How can a city dweller relate to God being a shepherd or a tabernacle or a rock? What does navigating adolescent angst have to do with "precious oil poured on the head, running down on the beard"[7] or the "dew of Hermon"?[8] And how do we even begin to explain the imprecatory psalms that talk of dashing infants against stones?

As you know, I grew up going to church. Our church's songbook was designed to make the singing of psalms a regular event. Each time one was announced it brought a (silent) groan from my brothers and me. My dad, who grew up singing lively hymns in another denomination, said singing psalms "felt like singing funeral music." I now realize that's not because of the psalms themselves but a lack of framing. Psalms themselves are the good stuff, treasures of faith.

So what do we say to orient novices to the psalms? As when framing the historic creeds and the Lord's Prayer, we regularly connect praying the psalms to our place in the worldwide church. Our simplest frame goes something like:

> We're now going to pray from the prayer book of God's people of all times and places.

A slightly expanded version we use:

> Sung and whispered, shouted and groaned by Muslims and Jews, Protestants and Catholics, Bob Marley and Bono and Bach, the psalms express the faith of a thousand generations. Let's pray one now.

These types of frames show we believe the psalms' particular language transcends time and place. To pray the psalms is to take up our voices with the global church:

> People of every continent and culture have used psalms to voice their deepest anguish and delight, to comfort and protest, and to express emotions they hardly dare admit. With the church around the world, let's pray one now.

These simple frames connect people to the Psalter as a whole. But what about times when you as an individual or congregation don't seem to feel the exact emotion of a particular psalm? Sometimes we simply name that reality. We acknowledge some in attendance may not be *feeling* the particular anguish of the psalm of the day, but in praying we show our solidarity with fellow believers and strugglers around the world:

7. Ps 133:2, NIV.
8. Ps 133:3, NIV.

Many of us have lived this week in relative comfort. We've had food to eat, shelter over our heads, and enough income to feel relatively secure. But there are people who have been hungry and homeless; some have been cheated, swindled, and beaten. Let's pray along with such people and on their behalf:

Or imagine tying this to a lifelong call:

Even monks get out of control. Their main job is to pray, but some floundered at this until the sixth century, when Saint Benedict wrote a *rule*, or guideline. In it he taught monks to pray the entire Psalter every week. But one phrase from Psalm 4 gets used every single day: Answer me when I call, O God of justice. It is not that the monks were consistently subject to injustice. It's that they are called to pray for the world. Let's join them.

It's a good gift to be repeatedly sent to *the* prayer book of worship, an action we believe prepares people to return in their private prayer as well. It also points them to *the* Person of the prayer book. Consider:

All through his life, in moments of faith and agony, on the cross and with his final breath, Jesus prayed the psalms. Following his lead, let's join in praying today's psalm.

In seasons like Lent, a specific psalm points us to Jesus so we can clearly know we are praying with him:

On the cross Jesus groaned in agony. Deserted and demeaned, hanging naked before the world, he expressed his anguish in words he'd likely learned as a child. Let's pray this psalm, Psalm 22, that Jesus prayed.

The psalms are a special treasure, lending themselves to many different frames, thick and thin, personal and historic. You might even (and we value this at our congregation) frame the specific psalm according to the worship element for which it is used. In this way the same psalm gets a variety of frames depending on its use as a call to worship, a prayer of confession, words of assurance, or a benediction.[9]

Maybe that's enough for now. I'm curious to hear a frame your group might design, maybe for this week's psalm.

With the whole church,
Kevin

9. I'm grateful for—and encourage you to listen to—an October 2012 presentation John Witvliet gave at Yale Divinity School, "Biblical Psalms in Christian Worship."

March

On Baptism

Dear Jordan,

You asked, with Easter Vigil coming soon, about baptism at our congregation. So many memories come to mind. Lives changed. Grace received. Like Jesse, who battled cancer for three heroic years. Our wise youth pastor visited Jesse every day of his last month of life. Only weeks before he was to die, this sixteen-year-old ex-football player, frail from months of chemo and radiation, asked to be baptized. He wasn't a churchgoer. Neither were his parents, or the grandparents who raised him from elementary school onward.

After fifteen years in our new building, his baptism is still the only time we've used our lift to raise someone to the height of our stage. After we waited in silence for his wheelchair to get to platform level, Jesse was wheeled to the front. His physique, once the flower of adolescent muscle and strength, was now a thin skeleton. Three weeks later he would be back on stage for his funeral.

Most often for baptism we bring in a tank for full immersion. Baptizands are dunked. Others who profess their faith, affirming the baptism of their childhood, step thigh-deep into the tank to remember their baptisms. But Jesse's body was too racked with cancer for a dunking. So we poured water on him as he sat bound to his wheelchair. And we baptized him in the name of the Father, and the Son, and the Holy Spirit.

What do you say to introduce or frame such a baptism? Few words were needed that day. We simply said:

> Baptism symbolizes our dying and rising in Christ.
>   It is a kind of dying, a drowning of our old self. A drowning of all our self-made plans and self-rule and self-sufficiency. Of all our own life choices.

And it is a kind of rising, a participation in the resurrection life of Jesus. A symbol that we are no longer our own, but his.

Today Jesse is baptized as a way of signifying his dying and rising in Jesus.

I know, and your group knows too, that baptism can feel like a great divide. Ironic, isn't it? A sacrament intended to bind followers of Jesus to each other and to him often splinters into clans of sharp opinions and uncompromising conviction. But in that moment, in the baptism of a dying adolescent, we saw its true meaning. We experienced firsthand the apostle's "one Lord, one faith, one baptism."[1] And those present that day will never forget.

In most baptisms, of course, the presence of dying and rising isn't so palpable. One Sunday morning we baptized a family of six young children. All were immersed, from oldest to youngest. All were absolutely enthralled by their own baptisms and the baptisms of their siblings. The youngest was only three months old. You should have seen the expression on his face as he emerged from the water. I've never seen a child quite as wide-eyed and alive with wonder. That time our frame accented the *belonging* of baptism:

> Baptism reminds us that we are not our own. We belong—body and soul, in life and in death—to our faithful Savior, Jesus Christ. He has fully paid for our sins with his precious blood. He watches over us in such a way that not a hair can fall from our heads without the will of our Father in heaven.[2] These children are now baptized to symbolize that they have entered into that promise of grace. What a way to grow up, to know you belong to God!

In our congregation, those being baptized or their parents answer questions based on a baptism formula from the third century. I have a friend from our same tradition who takes everyone outside to a nearby lake for baptism services. Before they baptize someone into their church and into the church universal, the entire congregation holds hands and wades into the water. Imagine him saying,

> We have a thousand identity options. Your primary identity can come from a political party or an ethnic group, from a social class or your economic status. You might inherit an identity from your parents or grandparents, choose one from a menu of options, or build your own with a lifetime of effort. But the

1. Eph 4:5, NIV.
2. Heidelberg Catechism, Q&A 1.

message of the gospel is that we receive our identity from Jesus. Baptism says our identity is a gift. We die with him. We rise with him. We all live under water.

My friend then moves into the deeper parts of the lake and baptizes folks to the cheers of those already wet with grace. I've framed it this way:

> We hear a thousand voices. Some voices condemn or belittle. Others flatter or cajole. Some insult or abuse. Voices tell us we belong or don't, that we're accepted or rejected. Some voices shout criticism; others whisper, "You'll never amount to anything." In baptism, we hear the one voice that matters. Because of Jesus, God whispers to us, "You are my beloved child, in whom I am well pleased." Hear that voice today—the baptism voice. And imagine that baptism voice shaping your identity for the rest of your life.

Baptism is a dynamic subject. It accents again how a frame can both connect a worship service to the historic, timeless church and be informed by local realities. We might suspect that a congregation in a Bible Belt state talks about this differently than one in a secular urban context. And here, of course, is another ideal opportunity to learn from those in your group who have other countries of origin. Your group will benefit from learning how baptismal practices are both like and unlike those in different countries. Knowing your group, with people raised in Nigeria, Afghanistan, India, and Cambodia, I can't wait to hear what you learn and practice. And no, I'm not sure a Chicago-raised "Cubs Nation" fan qualifies in the same way.

Enjoy what promises to be a fascinating conversation!

We are the baptized!
Kevin

On Membership Sunday, Baptismal Identity, and Inviting People to Belong

Dear Jordan,

It's Membership Sunday at your church? That's terrific. As you said, it's a wonderful reason to celebrate the stories of grace happening in your congregation. It's a gift, a time to pause and be grateful for God's grace so clearly at work. But I understand your concern, and that of your team. A conversation about church membership during a worship service can be bewildering and disorienting for folks both inside and outside the church. In our world of anti-institutionalism and deep reluctance to join anything, church membership feels like an outdated artifact.

You won't be surprised to know that we Californians struggle with framing it as well. Membership can feel to a first-time visitor like they've dropped onto an alien planet. A worship purist or attentive and reflective person might ask, "Did membership happen in the early church as well? And should we have membership now?" Is it a church treasure to be framed, or one of those alien practices that should be set aside?

A generation or two ago, many churches printed hymnals with thoughtful forms for membership, profession of faith, confirmation, and baptism. Such classic forms are themselves a kind of extensive worship frame. If you use these, or if you design your own, you'll likely want to introduce it with a custom frame. In our early days as a congregation, we framed it something like this:

> An old commercial tells us "membership has its privileges." In a world where we are reluctant to join anything, membership feels formal. Or foreign.
>
> But the Bible imagines every follower of Jesus as part of a community. Paul told a renegade narcissistic church that all Christians are *members* of one another.[3] He used the human body as a metaphor for the church. Individuals are members of a church like hands, fingers, and toes are parts of a body. They make diverse yet essential contributions to the whole.
>
> Membership in the church doesn't get you a special parking spot, a front row seat at the Christmas Eve service, or on a fast-track list of pastoral visits. Instead, it is a way to say and show you belong, that through baptism you understand every believer is a member of the universal church—the church of all times and places. In the next few minutes we will celebrate this belonging.

Now, almost three decades into congregational life, as we lean into the practices of the historic church, our former frame feels less satisfying. It captures the spirit of membership. But more and more we want to name how membership is really a living out of our baptism. So we say something like this:

> At the center of Christian life is baptism. Baptism is our first step of following Jesus, our first act of obedience. Through the centuries, the church has affirmed baptism by practices such as confirmation and profession of faith and church membership. All such practices are a way to live out and remember our

3. 1 Cor 12.

baptism, a way to take on and live our baptismal identity. And whether your baptism is in your past or in your future, in today's conversations we invite you to consider baptism as the center of your identity.

During such a service, our worship continues with questions, commitments, and baptisms. At the conclusion of this part of the service, those who have already been baptized receive, using water from the baptismal font, the sign of the cross on their foreheads. As we mark them with the cross we say the Aaronic blessing over them: "The Lord bless you and keep you; the Lord make his face shine on you and be gracious to you."[4]

We find it another instance of how a historic practice of the church can overflow with gospel joy. It's been a delight for people, and healing for many, to receive such a personal blessing in the context of worship.

I can already hear you saying, "These frames focus on baptism. Is there another way to go with membership?" Here is a frame that focuses on the church universal as a broken but grace-seeking community:

> Maybe you've noticed: The church is imperfect. It makes mistakes. Church insiders do and say embarrassing, even awful things. It is a family with embarrassing cousins and awkward relatives. Inside it have been charlatans, narcissists, manipulators, and hypocrites. Who would join such a group? (It makes me think of Groucho Marx's comment "I don't want to belong to any club that would accept me as one of its members.")[5]
>
> But Jesus says the church is also the salt of the earth and the light of the world. The Apostle Paul says it is the body of Christ, the bride of Christ, a collection of ambassadors, Jesus making his gospel known through us.
>
> This same group of Jesus-followers designed the world's first hospitals and orphanages. Church insiders started Alcoholics Anonymous, world relief agencies, and help for immigrants and orphans. And they are the single most financially generous group of people on the planet.
>
> Today, we have people standing before us who, knowing something of the church's brokenness and imperfection, dare to say, "I'm committing to Jesus." And also to his church.

What do you think? We find, as you are hearing in our conversation, it's often best to name and admit the broken reality of the church. But it's also helpful to point people to the clear (or obscure) way grace is also at

---

4. Num 6:24–25, NIV.
5. Johnson, "In Hollywood."

work. Our practice is to give church insiders and novices an understanding of how this event connects to the church universal, visible and invisible. You could also design frames that accent more directly the church's connection with fellow believers throughout the world. I'll be curious to hear what you decide.

Let me know how your celebration goes. I still remember the very first Membership Sunday at our church. We baptized twenty-three people that day. It was amazing.

Wishing you every grace,
Kevin

On Memorizing Frames (and Bible Readings)

Dear Jordan,

Thanks again for the invitation to join your team by video. I'm delighted to join your meeting electronically. It will be a wonderful gift to be together. After so many conversations back and forth and hearing about your team, I'm eager for us to see each other.

In the meantime, thanks for sending the video of your recent worship services. They're beautiful. So warm and heartfelt. So full of the gospel and grace. And so wonderfully thoughtful, gentle, and hospitable.

It's tricky to respond to your request for critique. Our team here, like football players and coaches, regularly reviews the video from our own worship services. Watching the service a couple of days later helps us see what we don't always see when we're actually in worship. We're often surprised at what we notice. And we've found it a valuable exercise. But the risk, as you know, is to reduce a worship service to a series of overly scripted plays, to a performance. Allow me two stories.

A few months ago I attended a friend's congregation in the Pacific Northwest. He's a wise pastor. It's clear he loves his congregants, and they love him. I wish you could have seen their warm impromptu pastoral prayers before communion. People come forward to pray with him or with an elder. Babies, toddlers, teenagers, families, and single friends all share heartfelt prayer. The body of Christ!

This pastor aims to do much of what we've been talking about in our conversations, framing worship for spiritual novices and veterans. He's smart. And hip. And dedicated. During several worship frames he looked at his congregation directly. But during others he read from his iPad, and that reading brought an edge of formality. I'm not trying so much to critique him (he really is a fine, thoughtful pastor, and I'd rather a worship leader prepare their in-between words carefully than wing it or not do them at all), but something is lost in the reading. The frame became more formal and official and less winning and winsome. I share this story to say that even the best of us are better when we are at ease, free to look people in the eye. As you've likely surmised, I'm encouraging you to internalize your worship frames. Even if you lose a well-crafted word or two in moving from reading to freely speaking, your demeanor will be far more personable. You're naturally winsome already; saying the worship frames without notes will let that warmth and grace naturally show in everything you do.

Here's the second story, about a wonderfully winsome friend. She's easily one of the kindest, most authentic Christian people I have ever met, and one of my all-time favorite people. Drop her into any setting, and she instantly has a raft of friends. Each week she greets people at the front door as they enter church. Maybe it's the warmth of her native Peru. Maybe it's her own contagious personality. Maybe it's a bit of both. But people actually stand in line to hug her before and after worship. Her naturally pastoral ability extends to her calls on folks who are sick or struggling. She's heartwarming!

So of course we wanted to include her on our worship leadership team. Our worship team hoped to impart that warm, personal touch. We gave her brief sections of the liturgy to start: a call to confession, a short prayer, an announcement, a worship frame. And because people love her, they are naturally drawn to her as a worship leader. But as a team, we could never quite enable her to be free as a worship leader, to speak with the same natural warmth she exudes before and after the service or during pastoral calls.

Together we wondered: why can't we empower her? Is part of this a language difficulty? As a native Spanish speaker, she at times can be self-conscious about her accent when speaking English. It's true that a few, especially older folks, occasionally say she's a bit more difficult to understand than other worship leaders. But the vast majority of us find her accent beautiful and endearing. Maybe it's because she left a more formal church as a teen, opting for a more vibrant, spontaneous style of worship? Is there something in the worship frames themselves that feels unnatural or formal to her? Maybe it doesn't work because memorizing is difficult for her? Whatever the reason (and we've worked together with her on this for more than two years), it's never quite felt natural to her.

In the end, she suggested, and we agreed, to let her worship leadership rest for a while. Maybe we'll revisit her participation in a few months. Again, I hope you hear the spirit of this. We're not critiquing her so much as we are working to name reality. I'd encourage your group to do the same. There are ways we can increase a person's capability in this area, but at other times we have to live with the mystery of God's unique gifting and calling.

I look forward to hearing the wisdom of you and your team.

Kevin

On (Skipping) Holy Week and the Journey of Faith

Dear Jordan,

Every Palm Sunday enthusiastic people tell me as they leave the worship service, "See you on Easter!" It feels as if they're announcing, "I don't do Holy Week."

We've found that participation in Holy Week is a formation journey— often a long one. Some people want an "Easter Jesus." They desire a faith that goes from victory to victory, success to success. The wisdom of the liturgical year as a whole, and Holy Week in particular, invites us into the whole of Jesus' life, including his suffering. Lent invites us to live reflectively, to remember the dying and rising symbolized in baptism.

Already during our congregation's first year we had a tenebrae Good Friday service—a reflective service of increasing darkness. At the time, our Sunday worship services included mostly upbeat songs, entertaining weekly children's messages, and dramas. In consideration of the spiritual seekers among us and in our neighborhoods, we celebrated communion at our Wednesday evening services. Good Friday services were somewhat inconsistent with our main worship practice. But as with many things, our wider church tradition—even if unintentionally—won the day. The tradition I grew up in was deeper in me than the innovative worship plans we followed week to week. You might even say that we unconsciously or subconsciously offered people an "Easter Jesus" with Good Friday being an anomaly.

Some churches we know stayed with the more innovative (we might say *frontier ordo*) worship pattern. Others did a sharp turn (or return) toward historic worship, giving attendees ecclesiastical whiplash. Our shift was slow and incremental. First we had monthly communion on Sundays, then biweekly, then weekly. In the same incremental way, we began following the liturgical year, starting with Advent, then adding Lent. Finally we let almost all our worship texts be dictated by the liturgical year.[6]

---

6. We follow the liturgical year very closely from Advent through Trinity Sunday. During Ordinary Time we often go verse by verse through a book of the Bible also used by the lectionary during that time.

Good Friday attendance was always sparse—maybe thirty percent of Sunday attendance.

As we slowly shifted back to historic worship, especially the liturgical year, we explored entering traditional practices of Holy Week. First, we added Maundy Thursday services, complete with foot washing. Over the years, our local church's tradition has been to have our youth groups lead the service. They do the readings and the music and help with the foot washing. Their leadership of Ash Wednesday and Maundy Thursday form a kind of Lenten youth tradition for us. I'm always struck by how meaningful the practice of foot washing is, even for first-time attendees.

For our twenty-fifth anniversary as a church, my parents flew from their home in Michigan to celebrate the milestone and participate in Holy Week. My mom was ill that evening and couldn't attend. But my dad, a church attendee for eighty years, had never participated in a Maundy Thursday foot washing. He didn't need to pass on to me his verbal evaluation; his tears said it all.

Three years ago we added Holy Saturday services. The poignant liturgy includes readings from Job and Lamentations. Maybe 5 percent of our congregation participated that first year, but it was an important step for us in further living out the formative power of worship .

The spirit of this service came into sharp focus last year when first-time attendees appeared in their Easter finest. They had assumed that we, like various other churches in our region, were having an Easter service that evening. We did our best to show them hospitality while staying faithful to the spirit of the service. I'm still curious how they processed the content of the service because they left and never returned.

We frame Holy Week in two ways. First, we frame each service at its beginning. For Maundy Thursday we say something like:

> Welcome to this Maundy Thursday service. On this night, we remember and celebrate the final supper Jesus shared with his disciples in the context of the Passover, when the people of Israel celebrated their liberation from slavery in Egypt. While in the upper room, Jesus washed the feet of his disciples and instituted the Lord's Supper. So today we think about self-giving love: Christ's for us, and ours for one another.

For Good Friday:

> Tonight, on Good Friday, we participate in a tenebrae service that reflects on Jesus' death and recalls the seven last things he said on the cross. As we remember his words, we will extinguish candles. The extinguishing will follow Bible readings, songs,

and prayers. Tenebrae services are quiet and reflective. Sit in the darkness, hear and sing the stories of Jesus' suffering, and then leave in silence.

For Holy Saturday:

> Welcome to this Holy Saturday service. Tonight we remember Jesus lying in the tomb, dead. Everything was still. You can almost hear the earth hold its breath, afraid to exhale. Tonight we wait. We lament. And we keep watch together.

Second, we frame the entire week. This may not need to happen in congregations or neighborhoods with a strong tradition (assumption?) of Holy Week practices. But in a community like ours, with dozens of traditions and novice believers, we need to frame what's happening. Sometimes during the announcements leading up to Holy Week we simply say,

> To fully appreciate Easter, we invite you to participate in the services of Holy Week as together we remember and follow the way of Jesus.

At other times we fill out the invitation a bit:

> During Holy Week the church remembers the great acts of our faith, specifically Jesus' dying and rising. We invite you to reflect on those events, and your own dying and rising, by participating in a series of worship services leading up to Easter. As one person told me last year, "I never really understood the depth of Easter until I participated in all these services."

Holy Week is a wonderful antidote to an "Easter Jesus"-only world. Sometimes I think those Christians who have kept these practices for generations are on to something!

Kevin

On Easter Surprise, and Dying and Rising

Dear Jordan,

You're so right. We've talked about this already, but it's well worth saying again: the Easter story is surprising on so many levels. So yes, that surprise can serve as the basis for a frame. You also asked about a possible frame using the story of Mary Magdalene. These two very good ideas have my mind whirring. Maybe they can work together? Consider:

What would you say if you'd just risen from the dead?

A pastor once asked a group of children this question.

One little girl burst out with, "Ta-da!"

When Jesus rises from the dead, his first word to Mary of Clopas and Mary Magdalene is "hello" (Matt 28:9). So simple, so profound, especially in a culture where "hello" also means grace and joy and peace. In the spirit of Eastertide, and as recipients of Easter love, let's pass the peace. Repeating Jesus' Easter welcome to centuries of Christians, let's greet each other with the resurrection life that promises grace and joy and peace.

As you suggested, it's a delight to play with the themes of Easter as a surprise beyond imagining and to infuse worship with that unexpected, delirious joy. How might you improve or tweak this shorter frame?

We see Easter as a date on a calendar. We can plan for it—or around it. But there were no plans that first Easter. Only a huge surprise. And it's still surprising when God sends his grace every Eastertide.

A few years ago, one of our worship leaders framed our passing of the peace on Easter Sunday like this:

The night Jesus died, his disciples fled. Terrified and unsettled, they deserted him in his hour of need, just as he predicted they would. Later, after they heard from some female friends what they took to be the rumors (nonsense) of Jesus' resurrection, they huddled together in a locked room. What should they do? Where should they go?

Jesus entered the room. And the first thing he said to them was "Peace." Isn't that still the first thing we want to hear from Jesus and from each other? With Christians throughout the world and centuries, we invite you to speak to each other the Easter words of Jesus, "The peace of Christ be with you."

I could also imagine an Easter frame about dying and rising, maybe the central image of the Christian life (and the liturgical year):

Christians disagree about a lot of things. Have you noticed?

How to vote.

When to be baptized.

Which music is best.

Whether to laugh in church.

How many Easter lilies are enough.

But we all agree that in Jesus' dying and rising, we also die and rise. His rising comes with a promise that one day we will rise too. Let us pray with that hope.

A few years ago one of my friends lost, between one Easter and the next, three of his family members. Racked with grief, he staggered into church ill-prepared and unready for soaring Easter anthems with ever-rising key changes. I wonder if, among the festive Easter pageantry and celebration, we should acknowledge the reality of loss:

> Jesus died. There was no mistake about that. And with him died his disciples' friendship, their hopes, their career aspirations, and their future. It's no wonder their response was to hide. To lock the doors. To keep everyone out. But suddenly Jesus was there, in the middle of their loss, their fear, their dread about what was next. Still today the risen Jesus appears to us, even when we keep everyone locked out. He is our hope. Let's pray to the risen Lord, who is present with us in our loss.

A local pastor named a new congregation Emmaus Road Church after that lovely Easter evening story where Jesus joins two of his followers as they walk an ordinary road home. Jesus acts ill-informed, seeming not to know even the events of his own life. It seems a moving Easter frame for communion:

> That first Easter evening, two friends walk home, dejected. On a road they've traveled a hundred times, their vision is clouded with grief. A stranger joins them. Earlier that morning, female friends had reported Jesus was risen. Supposedly Peter too had seen Jesus. But these friends hadn't. Or they couldn't, even while Jesus walked and talked alongside them. Only when Jesus broke the bread did they finally see him. Now, as we break the bread, as Jesus offers us his resurrected self, may Jesus make himself known to us.

In great Easter hope!
Kevin

April

On Ecumenical Creeds and Confessions

Dear Jordan,

I *love* that story! I can see your daughter now, standing as tall as her six years allow and pleading with her dad to make worship more meaningful to people her size and age. What a wonderfully earnest question from her. Knowing you, I'm sure you complimented her thoughtfulness and commended her question: "Why should anyone say a creed during a worship service?" A very good question—as is the one raised by your team when you first told them this story: "How can you in good conscience expect people to recite something they don't believe?" Apparently we are not finished hearing or asking questions!

I also value your firsthand description of the way reciting a creed felt puzzling to your neighbor during his first time visit to your worship service. It's terrific how the backyard conversation you had shows he trusts you enough to attend for the first time in his adult life! I do hope he comes back.

Maybe you've also talked with long-term Christians who find creeds equally off-putting, even a stumbling block to their sensibilities. Are you having those conversations too? We certainly are. It's no wonder, then, that in some churches creeds are viewed with suspicion, part of a collection of formal traditions or dubious teachings that squeezes out love for and understanding of the Bible.

We find that people with such questions are helped when we introduce or frame creeds with some brief historical background. As you know, creeds were used as a way to define and express truths about Jesus. We've found it useful to frame them in terms of that historical reality. For instance:

> Jesus is the most amazing, confounding, alarming, and captivating person ever to walk the planet. Even as the early church loved and worshiped Jesus, they found describing him beyond available words. Over time they assembled carefully formed

68

truths about Jesus into creeds. Creeds were one way to clearly describe and confess their faith in this most amazing person ever to live, and a way to invite novices into deeper understanding about who he is. We invite you to say a creed now as a way to enter into the mystery of Jesus.

Or consider introducing creeds with frames informed by another historical viewpoint. The early church used creeds to give spiritual novices reliable words to say about Jesus (and to keep them from heresy). Many Reformation-era confessions use them in this way, as teaching frameworks for the uninitiated, both children and adults. It would be ironic, then, for the sake of a spiritual novice, to exclude from a worship service the very thing the church historically used to teach and include people in the faith. With that in mind, what about a frame like this?

In the early church, spiritual novices memorized and spoke creeds as a way to take in the faith and to let it grow deep inside. At their baptism, new believers would say the creed as their first statement of faith. Veteran Christians would say it together to reinforce their own belief. In that spirit, whether you're a spiritual novice or a veteran, we invite you to say these ancient and time-tested words.

At times, a few words might emphasize the creeds' historic and global reference points:

It's wise to learn the words, practices, and rhythms of faith handed to us by our brothers and sisters throughout history. As pilgrims, together with those who have gone before us, let's say a creed the worldwide church has used since the early 300s.

Or how about this as another way to show solidarity with the universal church?

The church is not a place where we make up what we believe. It is a place where we receive the faith. In several places in the New Testament, the Apostle Paul used the word *paradosis* to talk about this faithful handing down of gospel.[1] Let's now, in the words of the Apostles' Creed, recite and receive the faith that has been handed down.

And maybe one more idea. Remember the creeds were born in a time of hot debate, when church leaders were trying to separate truth about Jesus from

---

1. 1 Cor 11:2; 2 Thess 2:15.

misguided half-truths. What if you allude to the difficulty of getting things *right* about Jesus?

> A long time ago, people were talking and teaching about Jesus in a way that wasn't in sync with the Bible. So church leaders got together and prayerfully and carefully wrote a summary of the basic truths of the Christian faith. Today we know it as the Apostles' Creed. Let's now say it together.[2]

Clearly you stoked my enthusiasm about this subject. I ended up giving you more examples than I first intended. I hope they get you started and especially that they help your neighbor. If you get a chance, I'd love to hear what you and your group might propose as a way to frame a creed. Imagine you are writing it specifically for your friend. That might help you start.

Grace and peace to you as you more fully take your place in the long line of those handing down the faith!

Kevin

On Historic Confessions

Dear Jordan,

This is a delight, sharing our ideas back and forth. Who knows, if we get good at this, someday we may write a book! Thanks for sending your group's idea for framing a creed. Let me make sure I have this right; it all got a bit garbled on the voicemail you left. Technology! Is this close?

> Every morning many of us reach for our smartphones. This everyday ritual reminds us that the world is alive and that we have a place in it. In a similar way, in the words of the Nicene Creed we remember God's care of the world and our place in it. I invite you to say this creed together.

There's a lot to like here. Its brevity, for one. Bravo! It's no small thing to introduce weighty ideas with a few simple words. And your frame is personal, accenting our relationship with God. At the same time, it accents the church as community, a place for spiritual vitality and growth.

If I were going to tweak it a bit (and forgive my over-analytical side here, but you *urged* me to give feedback), I'd encourage you to accent the communal nature of a creed more. Yes, on some level the church is a group of like-minded individuals. But so is the local bowling league or political party. We don't just say a creed; we *confess* it. And when we do, we are

2. Thanks to Sam Gutierrez for the foundation of this frame.

countercultural, insisting we cannot truly know Jesus by ourselves. Worship is personal, but it is not individual. It doesn't give people opportunity to form their own opinions about Jesus. The truth about him belongs to the global church. Via a creed, we speak our solidarity with Christians around the world at this moment and with those who have gone before us. I find it helpful to keep in mind the maxim of Cyprian, quoted by many followers of Jesus: "He cannot have God as a father who does not have the Church as a mother."[3] With that in mind, how might you tweak your first draft?

Again, let me say that I'm sure your frame was a gift exactly as you presented it. Which makes me wonder, did your friend, the self-proclaimed skeptic, attend again? And did he give you any feedback? I'd be curious to know what he thinks.

Glad to be in this together,
Kevin

P.S. I'm not sure this will come up in your congregation, but we find the historic creeds to be one thing and the confessions of the Protestant Reformation to be a different sort of challenge. They are not gifts of the church of all times and places but of a more specific time and place. Still, after use in many countries and languages, they are less parochial and more broadly tested than anything we could write today.

Here's a way we've found helpful for framing readings from one of our favorites, the Heidelberg Catechism:

> About five hundred years ago, when the truth of the Christian faith seemed uncertain and up for grabs, two twentysomethings got together and in a clear, sure voice articulated the historic faith. Let's recite their words—words that have brought comfort (and challenge) to Christians and congregations for centuries.

We've also found it helpful at times to introduce confessions in this way:

> As people of faith, we often find ourselves looking for words that clearly express our faith. It turns out Christians of other centuries and backgrounds searched for words as well—words that could explain the meaning of the Lord's Prayer and the Ten Commandments, of baptism and communion. Let's say words from a confession that give voice to the meaning of the Ninth Commandment.

---

3. Cyprian, *The Unity of the Church*, ch. 6.

On the Hallmark Calendar and Worship Wisdom
(National Holidays)

Dear Jordan,

Excellent question! Yes, Mother's Day is coming—and soon. And it comes with many competing expectations. For some congregations, it is second in festivities and impact only to Easter. Moms are honored, and they recruit even inconsistently attending children and spouses to participate in their Sunday. More than a few are also bribed with the promise of dinner out. What's a worship leader to do?

There are other secular holidays: Father's Day, Grandparents' Day, birthdays and anniversaries. But none has the import of Mother's Day.

Here's where the liturgical year and the secular (Hallmark) year seem wholly opposed. What if the lectionary text, usually Eastertide, Pentecost, or even Trinity Sunday, collides with an expected prayer and text honoring mothers?

I've learned there are at least two ways to go. One is to match the lectionary text with a theme of maternal love. After all, isn't every text a version of Jesus' greatest command—to love God and love people? Mothers are often the ones who best show us the way. As I type this, the lectionary gospel reading for the upcoming Mother's Day is John 14:1–14. In this passage Jesus assures his followers he has made a heavenly room for them and that he is the way. Imagine a frame that follows the lectionary and the holiday.

Another way to go is to directly acknowledge the complexity of Mother's Day. My wife, Gerry, and I were sensitized to this just before my first Mother's Day as a pastor. Graduate school was finished; we were settled in a new home and city. And right on schedule she got pregnant—a pregnancy that lasted ten weeks. Two more miscarriages followed. We won't forget the first Sunday after our miscarriage. Loving small-town Minnesotans in our church lined up to say an encouraging word. A few spoke well-meant but off-target attempts at encouragement that did more harm than good. But the great majority offered heartfelt, honest, painful, and personal stories: "We had a miscarriage too." "We were unable to conceive for years." "We are adoptive parents." "I lost my son when he was in junior high." More and more stories came. We were just getting to know this congregation, and they opened up their hearts and lives.

The episode gave us insight into this congregation overflowing with good and godly people. And it gave us insight into the startling complexities of parenthood. Mother's Day and Father's Day would never be simple festivities.

That first Mother's Day I stumbled on a prayer we've been using in various contexts for thirty years. I've seen it in a startling variety of churches. The complexity of motherhood is universal, as anyone who's read Bible stories about Sarah and Ruth and Bathsheba and Mary already knows.

Here's one version of this multi-decade prayer, introduced by the frame we used this past year while following the lectionary's Gospel texts for Eastertide telling stories of multiple post-resurrection encounters with Jesus. The frame:

> After Jesus rose from the dead, he met many people, always meeting them where they were. This morning, we honor mothers and pray that they would experience Jesus where they are. When I pray, "Gracious God," please respond, "Bless our mothers."

And the prayer:

> *Leader*: Gracious God,
>
> *Congregation*: Bless our mothers.
>
> *Leader*: We pause to recognize that for some of us, the word *mother* doesn't bring up memories of love and life. Instead, it brings up pain:
>
> The pain of the loss of our mothers.
>
> The pain of broken or abusive relationships with mothers.
>
> The pain of longing to be a mother but not being able to.
>
> The pain of lost children when being a mother was the hope.
>
> We recognize that words of blessing can seem foreign and frustrating.
>
> As you meet us in our pain, grant us your friendship and grace.
>
> Gracious God,
>
> *Congregation*: Bless our mothers.
>
> *Leader*: As we pray for our mothers, we thank you for those who have been
>
> faithful mothers, whether spiritual mothers or mothers by birth.
>
> Gracious God,
>
> *Congregation*: Bless our mothers.
>
> *Leader*: Thank you for mothers who have given us a place to call home, a place of safety and belonging in a world that can often feel so isolating and alien.

> Gracious God,
>
> *Congregation*: Bless our mothers.
>
> *Leader*: Thank you for mothers who have extended grace upon grace to us, who have given of themselves that we may live, just as Jesus gave of himself for our sake.
>
> Gracious God,
>
> *Congregation*: Bless our mothers.
>
> *Leader*: Today, we look to Jesus, who meets us as we are: sometimes full of pain, sometimes full of joy. Make us a church where those without mothers find them, where those who are mothers grow in grace, and where those who aren't mothers find the peace of your presence.
>
> Gracious God,
>
> *Congregation*: Bless our mothers. Amen.

Of course, something very similar can be said on Father's Day. Praying this prayer every year, we find we are taken again by the way this framing brings gospel grace to us as individuals and a community.

May our gracious God bless you,
Kevin

On the Bearing and Identity of Worship Leaders

Dear Jordan,

What a fine question from your group. I'm glad you have the kind of team where you value everyone's opinion. It's a treat to imagine you all in your worship space arguing and debating the merits of each position. It was curious to me how your team matched their particular stories—experience as a refugee, a doctoral candidate, an adoptee, a minority rights advocate, and someone who experienced regular homelessness growing up—to each person's favorite or suggested image of a worship leader.

You want me to weigh in on which I think is best? I can't. Or won't. The church has lived with a wide variety of images, and I'm sure your group can too.

Are you a shepherd? A priest? A spiritual parent? A pastor? An icon? A spiritual translator? A doctor of souls?

The church has adopted all of these titles in various times and places. And all have merit. I'd suggest two things. First, I'd steer clear of some images popular in some contemporary worship leadership. Your group didn't mention these, but they might know them. It became fashionable in the 1960s for pastors and worship leaders, maybe feeling a little out of place in meetings with lawyers and psychologists, to consider themselves professionals. Yes, okay, church leaders are professionals in the sense that professionals get paid for what they do, and in the sense that they are (we hope) competent and well trained, meeting certain established standards. Fair enough. But why not learn from the time-tested stance of the church? Why be a professional when you can be a doctor of souls?

In the same way, the idea of a worship leader as a verbal or musical performer lacks the depth of the time-tested wisdom of the church. Again, there's some value in the way the word *performer* suggests competence. We surely don't want incompetent worship leading. But can you hear in that phrase the assumptions that worship needs, by the leader's person or skill, to capture the interest of the attendees? Beauty in worship? Yes! But performance? No thanks.

It makes me think of what Martin Luther, who once chastised worship leaders, said:

> We have stuck to founding, building, singing, ringing, to vestments, incense burning, and to all the additional preparations for divine worship up to the point that we consider this preparation the real, main divine worship and do not know how to speak of any other. And we are acting as wisely as the man who wants to build a house and spends all his goods on the scaffolding and never, as long as he lives, gets far enough along to lay one stone of his house.[4]

Why be a much-loved entertainer when you can be a curer of souls?

Kevin

On Being Led by Learners or Experts

Dear Jordan,

So you're now talking about who is qualified, or called, to lead in worship? I was waiting for you to get to that. It's a tension every congregation experiences. Do you let a junior high student play her saxophone during the offering? How talented does a person need to be to play percussion in a

---

4. Plass, *What Luther Says*, vol. 1, 302.

worship service? Or the organ? Or to lead singing? And for that matter, how committed to the congregation and to the faith does a person need to be?

As you guessed, I've heard those questions before. And as you suspect, there are a variety of wise answers. The congregation you mentioned where they hire all professional musicians, believers or not, is one way forward. Their urban context makes professional musicians readily available and possibly even expected by congregants. A person could argue that this practice goes back to the Levites in Old Testament worship. By contrast, the church I served in Minnesota was a family that made room for everyone to do what they liked. How could a generous family not invite their much-loved fourth-grade son to play the piano at a family gathering? The joy isn't in the rendition or expertise, but in the relationship. In some congregations only ordained clergy lead worship; in others anyone who can play guitar or organ leads. There's more than one way. I'd suggest you talk about it as a worship team. Might it be helpful to write a policy and send it to your church leadership team for input and approval? It could be of short- and long-term benefit to have clarity on this as a congregation.

As for our tête-à-tête on worship frames, let me suggest that anyone can try to create them. While some congregations might have a gifted word-smith they habitually rely on to design and lead frames each week, it's easy to imagine a group like yours doing this as part of its communal work.

Come to think of it, the exercise itself might be a useful discipleship tool. Imagine each of your team members coming to your next worship planning meeting with an example in mind. You could assign them various worship elements or let them choose. You might then process these examples as a group. Ask some questions. Have some fun. Why do some work more than others? Which ones are especially hospitable to spiritual veterans? How do they include people of multiple generations and backgrounds? Which one would you want to use this Sunday?

Couldn't we even imagine a similar exercise for the non-worship planners? Imagine a church-wide conversation about worship where one of the exercises is to design these frames. Imagine an elder or deacon meeting where everyone writes and evaluates sample worship frames. And couldn't the high school and junior high groups try the same thing? Awareness of each worship element would be enhanced, as would a desire to value and implement church-wide hospitality.

Okay, so now I've gotten worked up about my own idea. I can hear you saying, "It's not the first time." Fair enough! But let me know what you think. And while you're at it, for the sake of our conversation, send me some frames you're working on.

Have fun,
Kevin

May

On Pentecost, National Identity, and Jesus as Our True Home (Global Church)

Dear Jordan,

We remember that Jesus and the disciples spoke in the vernacular. They spoke in ordinary words, in the language of the people. Church historians note the transition in Bible translations from medieval Latin to the languages of the people. Mission theorists document how translation work in the last hundred years revitalized many world cultures and preserved some local languages from extinction.

The Holy Spirit speaks in the vernacular, in the language of the common people. It's no wonder, then, that on the day of Pentecost, every person gathered heard about God in their own language. That's good news.

Explore the vernacular in global Christian worship.

A friend of mine born in South Korea now lives in California. One day he told me he considers himself a misfit. I was surprised because each week after worship—a service he helps lead—he stands in the atrium surrounded by friends in laughing banter or reveling with the grade school students he helps teach. A misfit? I protested, pointing out his trendy phone, hip jeans, cultural lingo, and many friends. He acknowledged his multicultural aptitude but explained, "In my native language I'm funnier. My jokes are better, my stories more entertaining, and everyone 'gets me.'"

Still I objected. "You fit."

He nodded, but said, "All immigrants are misfits."[1]

Pentecost celebrates the rich heritage of our nations-loving God. Knowing that, how might we celebrate and frame Pentecost worship? How do we sing and pray with an awareness of the way God treasures and designs all peoples? This frame taps into the Old Testament flavor:

1. Adapted from Adams, "Scythian Worship?"

78

All through the Old and New testaments, God identifies himself as the God of *all* peoples. All nations come to him (Ps 47 and 72). Abram is renamed Abraham, the father of *many* nations (Gen 17). Isaiah tells us that at the end of all things, when in God's amazing grace Jesus returns to make all wrongs right, nations and people won't lose their cultural identity. Instead, it will be *redeemed* (Isa 66:18–19). While Israel is God's chosen nation, the identity is not designed to promote ethnic pride or privilege, but to be a call to representing and extending God's love to all peoples. Each nation has a place in God's geography. Knowing that, let's sing this multi-language song of worship.

Or what if we accent the Pentecost flavor of Jesus' family heritage?

Included on Jesus' family tree is Ruth the Moabite, Rahab the Amorite, and Bathsheba, the wife of a Hittite. Jesus talks extensively with a Samaritan woman. Is it no accident that we read about his disciple Philip explaining the gospel to an Ethiopian eunuch, or that a Roman centurion says after Jesus' death, "Surely this man was the Son of God."[2] Today, on the feast day of Pentecost, we celebrate God giving his Holy Spirit to all people. Let's pray.

Or we might think of a frame with a personal or cultural emphasis:

Knowing Jesus doesn't flatten our national or cultural identities. The missional hope of the Bible is not in wiping out nations, but to have them become fully alive, to help us experience what historian Lamin Sanneh said about the gospel coming to his West African neighborhood: "People sensed in their hearts that Jesus did not mock their respect for the sacred nor their clamor for an invincible Savior, and so they beat their sacred drums for him until the stars skipped and danced in the skies. . . . Christianity helped us become renewed Africans, not re-made Europeans."[3] At Pentecost we celebrate that the Bible is good news for all people. In that spirit, and remembering the dazzling international flavor of the church, let us celebrate the Eucharist.

Or this Eucharist invitation:

In a balkanized world where politics, ethnicity, and nationalism vie to be our main identity, Pentecost reminds us we belong first to Jesus and to his community, which spans all times and all

2. Mark 15:39, NIV.

3. Sanneh, *Whose Religion Is Christianity?*, 43.

places and includes misfits from every continent. In this new community, people who are typically pushed to the side or kept on the margins—immigrants and aliens and people stuck in poverty—find a new expression of their humanity and belonging. Pentecost joins slave and free, Greek and Jew, male and female, American and Canadian, Korean and Japanese, Russian and German, Nigerian and Honduran into one family. In that Pentecost spirit, let us commune with our redeeming God and his people around the world.

Pentecost reminds us that in Jesus no one is a misfit.

Yours,
Kevin

On Ordinary Time

Dear Jordan,

This past week after our worship service, a new attendee came up to me and asked, "What is Ordinary Time?" As you know, it's simply the season of the church year without the big feasts like Christmas, Easter, or Pentecost. It's a time when ordinary followers of Jesus remember to live their ordinary lives. Maybe that's the frame. What do you think of that? We might also consider a frame like this:

> So much of the life of following Jesus is daily. Sure, there might be memorable moments and big decisions; and there are seasons of intense happiness and pain. But much of following Jesus is ordinary. This can come as a surprise to people new to the faith, who sometimes expect fireworks every day. But wise Christians shaped a liturgical year that not only celebrates big feast days like Christmas and Easter, but also a long season they called Ordinary Time. Ordinary Time is a season when we simply follow Jesus in routines—we show patience, kindness, generosity. We live out our faith in routine discipleship. We live in and do the work of our community. We participate in the mission of God. And we remember we belong to the people of God. This all seems so ordinary. And it is. But so is the following of God's Spirit.

I'd be curious to know what you think of the frame. I think it's okay, but a bit too long. Shorter is almost always better. It feels not quite fully baked. And it needs a fresh chef to see if it has all the right ingredients—or too many. How would you adjust it? Or, at the risk of pushing the image too far, how might you cook it up or customize it for your congregation?

Right this moment I'm tempted to add another ingredient, a sentence saying Jesus lived most of his life in Ordinary Time. So did Mother Teresa. So do all of us.

Ordinarily yours,
Kevin

On Trinity Sunday

Dear Jordan,

I know. No one on your team wanted to be the point person for Trinity Sunday. You'll have to talk to the good folks who were assigned Advent and Epiphany. They thought their task was a challenge, but they weren't charged with clarifying the Trinity! I understand your bewilderment about where to start. Who can explain the Trinity? And in just a few sentences? Take heart that it took the church a few centuries to put words on that too. In fact, maybe that's a good frame:

> Look for the word *Trinity* in the Bible and you won't find it. But today is Trinity Sunday. We celebrate God as Father, Son, and Holy Spirit. To celebrate the Trinity doesn't mean we understand the mystery. It took the church 300 years to begin to put words on the mystery of God as three in one. But we do know God is divine, loving, life-giving community. And that is worth celebrating.

Or how about this:

> In a moment, we're going to join followers of Jesus around the world and throughout the ages in reciting the Nicene Creed. This creed was formed as a way to describe the idea of God as Holy Trinity—as three in one. As we celebrate Trinity Sunday today, notice how the creed celebrates God as divine community.

Or even:

> God is love. The sentence sounds so basic. It's an assumption everyone seems to share. But how could one person be the definition of love all by themselves? Today we celebrate Trinity Sunday, meditating on the fact that the Father, Son, and Holy Spirit are a singular community of overflowing, generous love for all eternity.

Once, while writing a paragraph for an assigned essay, one of my students, a youth ministry major at a Christian college where I teach, said, "It doesn't matter if my high school students know about the Trinity. I only want them to get to know Jesus." I hope his essay was only a quick and thoughtless answer to the assignment, because can anyone, adolescent or otherwise, know Jesus without also knowing the Father and the Holy Spirit?

I'm sympathetic to my student. Most Protestant churches rarely mention God as triune. It makes me appreciate our Roman Catholic and Orthodox friends who frequently pray in the name of the Father, Son, and Holy Spirit. Come to think of it, that's a kind of frame.

In the name of our triune God,
Kevin

P.S. Do you know that a favorite trinitarian image of the early church is given in the word *perichoresis*? The basic idea is that the Father, Son, and Holy Spirit are in an eternal, mutually life-giving, contagious dance of delight and mission. What do you think about writing a frame on that?

On Printed and Projected Frames

Dear Jordan,

I love it! What a fine, and dare I say obvious, point.

If we frame *every* worship element, a worship service gets unwieldy and needlessly wordy. Well-intentioned framing overdone can transform an amazing art gallery into a storage room overstuffed with clutter.

One of my graduate students was recently named pastor of a historic church. Feeling the effects of decades of decline, the congregation made a courageous final step. Rather than close their doors, they gave themselves to a thriving congregation in their region to be a mission outpost. And by the grace of God, he was named pastor of that site. You'd like David; he overflows with missional energy and passion. He loves his neighbors and is unafraid to tell them so. He's a refreshing and hopeful change for this site.

He and I talked about framing, both in a class on worship and in one on spiritual formation. A gregarious person and a capable student, he took to the idea of framing immediately, instantly seeing its use for making known the unknown. Months into his new charge, he told me that he and his congregation were happily framing their worship. But, he said almost as an afterthought, because of the frames, the service was getting, in his words, "quite a bit longer." He assumed extended service times were an essential aspect of framing—adding words to the liturgy takes more time. But on hearing his assumption, I quickly named what you're discovering. Not every element needs to be framed every week. Yes. We are tracking!

One possibility is, in your words, to rotate which element gets a frame. Another possibility (and many congregations do this already) is to print some frames on a handout or show them via an overhead projector. Growing up we called this handout the church bulletin. Full of information, it specified the meeting times of various groups, the contact names for standing committees, and the details of upcoming events. It also included an order of the worship service—a section of the bulletin mass-produced yearly since it never changed.

A couple of years ago I attended a worship service in a remarkable Episcopal cathedral in Portland. As I entered, an usher handed me a twenty-page, full-sized handout. The first seventeen pages of this communiqué featured every word to be spoken or sung, including musical notes. It was a masterpiece. Clear and elegant, simple to follow. I know your setting enough to surmise you may not want to add a twenty-page printout to your services. But maybe we can still learn from them?

After experimenting with various options over the years (paperless worship, projecting musical notes, and the like), we've settled on a hybrid setup. Songs, certain prayers, and various artistic images are projected on the screen. But there's also a printed handout that includes the names of various elements, song titles, and a guide to communion.

And "guide" is the operative word. It may seem picky, but in the name of communicating clearly we call this printed handout a Worship Guide. Of all the things it does, the most important is to guide (and frame) worship. Semantics can matter.

This guide is referenced at the beginning of the service as a help for novice attendees. To shift images a bit, a printed worship guide can be a kind of map for moving forward. It can provide orientation to the basic landmarks of this new experience called worship. Here's what we put in our worship guide about communion:

> Communion is the family meal of Christians. We invite all followers of Jesus to participate. We celebrate using the historic practice of intinction. Someone will hand you a piece of bread and say, "The body of Christ for you." You can receive it and perhaps offer the words "Thanks be to God." Then someone will place a goblet in front of you so you can dip the bread in the wine. They will say, "The blood of Christ for you." Again you may say (if you like), "Thanks be to God." If you are not participating today, we invite you to come forward to receive a

blessing. Simply come forward in the communion line and cross your arms.

It's maybe a bit long. We'd love you to send us an edited version. But newcomers have found it helpful. Here's what that historic Episcopal cathedral printed about communion:

> All who are drawn to God are welcome to receive communion at Trinity. After the priest prays from the altar, everyone is invited to come forward. You may stand or kneel to receive the bread (wafer) in your hands and drink the wine from the cup. If you'd prefer to have the communion server intinct (dip) your bread in the cup, please leave it in your open hands. If you'd prefer not to receive but would like a blessing, cross your arms over your chest.[4]

Their guide also coaches worshipers on the way their congregation prays with a paragraph that says:

> Episcopalians pray with our whole bodies! In general, we stand to sing, sit to learn, stand or kneel to pray and cross ourselves as a sign of blessing. However, the Episcopal Church encourages a wide variety of devotional practices, so please join in as you are moved to, and don't worry about making a mistake.[5]

As a first-time attendee more familiar with other Christian worship rituals, I was struck by the warm, succinct, pastoral invitation to join in their historic practice, to authentically bring myself, letting go of any anxiety about getting it wrong. Their hospitality was real and unmistakable. They were expecting newcomers like me, clearly *hoping* we would attend. And they put their welcome in writing. What a gift.

In our neighborhood, the part of the worship service arousing the most suspicion is the offering. Newcomers are wary and guard their wallets from sweet-talking religious charmers. So our printed worship guide frames our offering like this:

> We receive two offerings each week. The primary offering goes toward sustaining the life and work of our church. The monthly mission offering goes toward mission causes inside and outside the church. It rotates monthly.

Multiple people have told us they appreciate the way these simple sentences put them at ease.

4. Trinity Episcopal Cathedral, "Welcome to Trinity Episcopal Church."
5. Trinity Episcopal Cathedral, "Welcome to Trinity Episcopal Church."

Of course, I'd love to hear what you think of this. Can printed frames orient newcomers in a way that coordinates with spoken words? Does your church do such a thing? If so, please send copies.

Much grace to you!
Kevin

P.S. Another advantage of a printed frame, besides keeping spoken frames from overburdening the service, is that many among us get anxious or unsettled if they don't know the order of events in advance. A printed guide can be a grace to them.[6]

---

6. For more ideas about universal design in worship and shaping worship for people of various abilities, visit allbelong.org.

June

On Framing the Service as a Whole

Dear Jordan,

As we described during Holy Week, sometimes it's helpful to frame the worship service as a whole. Think back to the story about Benjamin guiding our family through Westminster Abbey. Before he helped us see (framed) the individual treasures of the great landmark, he oriented us to the Abbey as a whole. A few words about its founding and purpose, its history and architectural sensibilities, helped us better see and take in all the treasures inside. A word about the whole helped us appreciate the parts.

One of my friends, a church planter in a secular urban setting, does this every week. Before a word is spoken, a prayer is prayed, or a song is sung, he welcomes everyone with these words:

> Welcome! It is a delight to have you here. No matter what your previous church experience, or lack of church experience, we hope today's worship service will be a gift to you. Our hope is that you will have a thoughtful and joyful encounter with God's grace. Our worship follows the historic pattern used in Christian worship for 2,000 years.

There are endless variations on this, of course. One is to have this overall orientation happen in the middle of the service rather than at the beginning. Returning to the example of Benjamin at Westminster, imagine if he guided us to individual treasures and then, after we'd experienced these riches, directed us to take in the larger perspective that held these treasures together.

Our congregation almost always offers an overarching frame in the middle of our worship service when we make a few brief announcements and invite children to go to age-appropriate teaching venues. We speak words that begin to prepare people for participation in the Eucharist that ends our service. One of our worship leaders points people to our printed worship guide, where they can find an explanation of who should participate in communion and how:

> Welcome again to Granite Springs Church. We are delighted you are here. Even if it's your first time, we hope you will get a sense of belonging, and of the grace of God. As a way to experience grace, we invite you to join us for Eucharist, which will immediately follow the sermon. You're invited to participate.[1]

Maybe this is a good time to return to our wayfinding image. Ancient cathedrals were designed to tell and reinforce the story. The soaring architecture, the stained glass windows, the sculptures, and the side chapels are visual signs that guide worshipers and support the biblical story.

Great art galleries do that too, don't they? The Louvre in Paris, the Metropolitan Museum of Art in Manhattan, the Guggenheim Museum in Bilbao, Spain, the Borghese gallery in Rome—all use elements of space and light to help visitors experience the art treasures together.

Framing friends together,
Kevin

On Singing and Unhelpful Impromptu Frames

Dear Jordan,

I know what your pastor means. I feel her pain—acutely. So do preachers everywhere. She worked on her message all week. Labored. Edited. Modified it from a myriad of possibilities down to the final draft. She spent extra time on the conclusion. She wanted the sermon to end memorably, like a well-crafted symphony or a movie that leaves you inspired. And as soon as she finished, the music leader rose to ad-lib a song introduction ranging over several unrelated topics before you actually got to singing. Here is an example of that kind of unhelpful frame endured by congregations:

> Isn't that a great message we just heard? It reminds me of a story I heard this week on my favorite podcast. It's about one of my favorite musicians, a little-known soloist from Lithuania. And it fits with a new song I've been working on all week. It expresses what I was feeling Tuesday morning and what I think a lot of us feel week to week. It doesn't have much to do with the sermon

---

1. Granite Springs Church, *Worship Guide.*

we just heard, but is authentic to my heart's ups and downs this week.

Okay, you got me. My layers of frustration got the best of me. This caricature is unfair. But I'd also contend that unhelpful, unplanned worship frames—especially before songs—are far too common.

And to answer your question, yes, it's worth talking to your music leader directly. Some musicians feel obligated to say something at various points in the service, as if it's their duty to speak words of transition. So it's worth clarifying. It's likely that in the sermon's conclusion your pastor said everything that needed to be said to frame or introduce the song that followed. If the music leader didn't know a frame was coming (especially one that's undesired or unneeded), he may have spent much of the sermon internally drafting an impromptu one. What if instead both preacher and musician weigh the best options in advance of the service? This might be a time to say it's often helpful for team members to prepare their worship frames in advance and to submit them for group feedback. Not only does such pre-service conversation sharpen and improve individual frames, but it also helps clarify various expectations between leaders. For most worship services, it's best to have only a few of the elements framed.

Most of the time, our experience suggests, framing for songs is best kept to one sentence. Remember the skilled framing of the art museum docent who says with astonishing simplicity, "Look for all the paintings with a significant contrast between light and darkness." She didn't explain every detail. She simply and elegantly stirred and prepared your imagination. Your ability to see and experience the paintings was skillfully cued. You've heard songs framed well too:

> Today we're going to sing this song in solidarity with our sisters and brothers in China, home of the fastest-growing church in the world.

Or imagine a worship leader saying Tish Harrison Warren's words:

> Christians are singing people. From ancient monks chanting the Psalms to Wesleyan hymnody, music has always been a way for the church to hone its theology and practice prayer with artistry and beauty. On every Sunday in every corner of the earth you can find Christians singing. From Gregorian chant to African American spirituals to acoustic worship bands to Syriac chant to East African kwaya, we hear music echoing from every gathered community of Christians.[2] Let's sing together.

2. Warren, *Liturgy of the Ordinary*, 133.

Several years ago I was able to visit the Cathedral of Santiago de Compostela in Spain. It's one of the three main pilgrimage sites of medieval Europe, with Rome and Jerusalem. For centuries pilgrims have walked El Camino de Santiago (the Way) for weeks and months as a spiritual and physical journey. A friend of our family spent three months walking it from Paris. Each day a Pilgrim's Mass celebrates the pilgrims and their Lord. Before the service began the day we visited, a tiny nun rose to the dais and spoke to us in broken Spanish, urging us to prepare for the singing that would follow. After encouraging us with words, she led by example, and the music that came out of this diminutive nun stunned us. Sweetly, powerfully, her music soared over the pilgrims and their backpacks, the regulars and the tourists. She simply said to us, "Muy alto," her way of encouraging us to sing louder. Like generations of song leaders before her, her main frame was her embodied example and, in her case, two words—words that inspired a song that rose to the top of that time-worn cathedral and echoed exquisitely between its stone walls. Two words told us all we needed to know.

Here's to harmony,
Kevin

P.S. No, I don't think one sort of worship music is more appropriate than another. A church I know started a ministry at a local truck stop and what they called "cowboy music" was just the thing. A congregation that meets on a beach in Hawaii may well have music influenced by its environment, just as Saint Paul's Cathedral in London will likely feature the best English hymnody and a Cuban congregation might be influenced by salsa. My encouragement has two parts. First, pay attention to the song diet of your congregation. Does it feature lament as well as praise, local and multinational songs, recent and historic? To put it one way, will the songs you're singing last for at least two or three generations? And, because worship songs are formative, are the lyrics worth singing to a person on their deathbed? Fitting our theme of worship frames, are the lyrics intelligible to secular people? Some biblical ideas need introduction. But much of what enters worship as contemporary lyrics is as unintelligible as the tongue speakers Saint Paul describes in 1 Corinthians 14. How much better to sing lucid lyrics that invite someone deeper into grace!

On Confession: Groveling, Grace, and the Actualized Church

Dear Jordan,

I love it! Your team is off to a good start. As we walk through a sample service together, I'm so taken with the frames you're creating. What you sent is just right—simple, brief, and packed with superb hospitality. It's great as is. And maybe, since you all asked for feedback, I might enter your group conversation and offer a simple tweak or two. What about this? I changed only three words:

> When we confess our sins, we are not groveling in guilt, but dealing with it. In the next few moments, in what we call confession and assurance, we honestly face the ways we've contributed to the mess of the world, and we hear God's good news of forgiveness.

It's a wonderful example of a worship frame. And it's wonderful to learn that two of your team members spoke these words together, alternating between English and Pashtu and Dari, bringing to mind places where the world seems especially messy. I can see why many in your congregation were moved to tears. There was nothing rote or overly formal; instead your entire congregation saw again the amazing treasure of confession the assurance of forgiveness because of the adept way you framed it. It makes me look forward to the next frame your group will create. What delight. Can you send me several others?

You asked me to share some of our frames for confession as well. You'll see some variety based on the authors of the frame and their own personalities. A gregarious, much-loved, long-term member of our church wrote this:

> As I look at you this morning, you're above average in about every way. You're articulate and interesting. You're smart and funny. You're honorable family members and dedicated community citizens. It seems we have hardly any faults. Or is it just that we'd rather not have any exposed? We'd rather not have our secrets publicized, or our diary read aloud, or our inept blunders made public. We'd rather be *covered*. The miracle of grace is that God *has* read our diary and our social media—and God loves us anyway. Each week we get to hear good news again from the God who has our sins covered. Let's confess and pray to God.

A few months ago, one of our newest team members, a college student double-majoring in English and philosophy, wrote this. It shows her interests and background, but she framed confession in a way that touched the human experience of us all:

> In his book *Being and Nothingness,* John Paul Sartre imagines one of us looking through a keyhole. He can see people and their idiosyncrasies, their unwatched and unguarded moments. It feels delicious because they are unaware he is watching. Few things feel as powerful or satisfying as being an unwatched watcher. But suddenly he hears a noise and realizes someone is watching *him.* Someone sees the delight he experiences in being an unviewed viewer, and he feels a kind of nakedness.
>
> We work hard to market ourselves. On social media and in routine conversation, we airbrush our own stories. We master image management. The thought that someone sees us—with complete access to our thoughts and words and behaviors—is beyond bearing. Unless it's God. Today we remember again that God sees us. And knows us. And, by the miracle of God's grace, *loves* us.
>
> Let's confess our sins and hear his assurance.

This frame is big. It's thick. It may be almost as long as the actual words of confession and assurance. Most of the time a thin frame is optimal. People lose interest quickly. And, as we've said, most often worship leaders need to pull back from being verbose. But, sometimes, infrequently, a thick frame is just the thing. Especially if it's extra poignant or has a surprise. This frame's unusual start and arresting style captured our attention and made confession real.

Maybe that's enough confession for now?

Or maybe, while we're on such a fascinating subject, just a few more? It's hard to imagine, isn't it, that we can be so excited about confession of sins? Yet it really is one of the treasures of the church at worship. As you know, one of my favorite authors on worship is the Russian Orthodox priest Alexander Schmemann. One bitterly cold morning at a student mission conference in Ohio, Schmemann, an enthusiastic proponent of worship, said the church is *actualized,* or "becomes itself," during the liturgy. In worship, not only do receive the means of grace in preaching and in the sacraments, but we become who we are as the redeemed. In confession and assurance, we do not mindlessly repeat a formulaic prayer; we *become* the forgiven and the forgiving.

You asked for more samples of our frames for confession and assurance, as if you can't get enough! Like I said, the great majority of the time we use a thin frame, a simple orientation, but our team recently used another thick one. It's an introduction our worship leader designed a few months ago. It was just after part of an earthen dam eroded a hundred miles north of us and thousands of people evacuated to our city. It's an example of how a frame can be both timely and timeless:

> There are so many places in life we want to be *covered*. We worry about health insurance. We call it Covered California, but when we feel a lump on our body we think, really? Am I covered? A dam threatens to break, and we load our most precious possessions into the car and join thousands of people on a wearisome six-hour trip to higher ground and think, am I covered? Our best friend has the dirt on us. We confided in him too quickly. And now he knows our foibles, our weaknesses, our social gaffes.
>
> It feels like we're going through life wearing a hospital gown that doesn't close well in the back. We can't stand to be uncovered, and we'll do almost anything to run back to the hospital sheets. The ancient practice we call confession and assurance reminds us that we are covered—not by our own skill, but by the grace of God.

Here's another thick frame in the same spirit. We haven't used it yet, but one of our team just sent it to us for review and feedback. I'm taken by it, and wonder if it might also work in your context.

> Some of us are experts at spin. A junior high teacher shows her class an R-rated movie and simply tells parents, "Mistakes were made." An athlete tests positive for performance-enhancing drugs and says, "My physician gave me the stuff, and I didn't know what it was." It's as if we never outgrow "The dog ate my homework." It's my wife's fault I had an affair. It's my accountant's fault my books are a mess. We spin. We point the finger. We assign blame. We pull the wool over our own eyes.
>
> Most of us are pretty accomplished at image management: we duck or dodge or misdirect with the best of them. But we carry nagging doubts. Have we done enough?
>
> There is another way. Imagine a week or a year or a life with no need to spin or deceive or misdirect or dodge. Wouldn't it be great if God's own self would cover us? If we knew we were completely accepted by God? That's the promise we are given in these next moments of confession and assurance. Confession is a chance to speak, to hear the open, honest truth, and to let God forgive us.

During Lent, we used a frame to introduce confession and assurance that spoke directly and meaningfully about the crucifixion itself.

Crucifixion was the worst kind of death invented at the time. Victims were exposed, mocked, and stripped naked. The goal was complete humiliation. A person's arms were spread out and tied or nailed down. Often a victim's legs were broken so he couldn't push up to gasp for air. The crucified didn't die quickly, but slowly. They didn't die privately, but publicly. Often, they would simply die of exposure.

Today in our confession and assurance, we remember that Jesus was stripped so we could be clothed. He was mocked so we could be loved. He was exposed so we could be covered. God counted Jesus a sinner so God could count us as redeemed. Let us confess our sins and receive this costly grace.

What very good news that we are redeemed,
Kevin

On Psalms and Mission

Dear Jordan,

Did I really mean that psalms are hospitable and not *in*hospitable?
Yes.

I know they can feel disorienting, like riding a roller coaster in the dark, full of abrupt twists and startling corkscrews. One moment the psalmist is lost in inner praise or silent reflection, and the next he calls down judgment on God's enemies (Ps 139) or he expresses his piety and then continues to pray that scheming people will fall into the traps they set for others (Ps 143).

This disarming honesty is what makes the psalms so contagious and hospitable to all sorts of faith stages and realities. I have a friend from Pakistan who argues the psalms are a way for Christians to connect with Muslims—think of that!—by helping them connect the gospel with their culture's poets. Because Islam honors David as a prophet, Muslims might sing psalms. It's certainly true that the psalm writers deeply held the idea that their God is for everyone. I wonder if we might incorporate that into our frames?

When I was a child, our entire Sunday school class learned Psalm 100. It is a beautiful psalm of thanksgiving, and that's in part why we pray it today. But think of the audacity of the original writer. From their tiny, often overrun country, the psalmist declared their God is the true God. For everyone. Imagine "Shout for joy to the Lord, *all* the earth." Let's pray with that same thankful expectancy.

Or try this frame for Psalm 67:

> God's people are always invited to revel in and receive God's
> blessing. God turns God's face to us and shines God's smile. God
> blesses us so we can invite others into God's blessing and into a
> life of flourishing. Let's pray for this vision of global thriving.

The psalms are saturated with this global mission orientation and mo-
mentum. The vision of the Psalter is the worship of the God of every nation.
Sometimes the desire for global flourishing is an open declaration, as in
Psalms 67 and 100. At other times the missional invitation is more personal.
Such psalms invite individuals inside to voice their objections to belief and
to acknowledge the difficulty of trust, all the while providing words to express doubt *inside* the faith. Though they seem to be contrary ideas, mission
and doubt go together. The psalms are mission-minded not *despite* voicing
doubt, but *because* they voice doubt—the universal experience of faith.

Psalms are hospitable and accessible to every person because of their
unfailing and unvarnished honesty. Psalms (and this is why our conversation naturally connected psalms to human story) assure us that no one
needs to neatly organize their faith before they can enter. Instead, all are
welcome to enter, even with our tangle of emotions, hopes, and anxieties,
to voice them in covenantal speech. Thank you, writers and editors of the
psalms! What do you think of this frame?

> Life is disorienting. Often the line between faith and doubt
> seems blurry. People on the inside of faith have doubts, even if
> they don't name them. And people who think their doubt keeps
> them on the outside of the faith have an urge to pray or a yearn-
> ing to trust that surprises them. Thankfully, the psalms invite us
> to pray this tangle. So whether you're a doubting believer, a be-
> lieving doubter, or somewhere in between, we invite you to pray.

We've discovered that people who doubt appreciate the hospitality. It
reminds me of the title of a famous sermon Harry Emerson Fosdick gave at
Asbury Seminary, "The Importance of Doubting Your 'Doubts.'"[3]

Psalms know what we and our spiritually seeking friends can know
too: that all of us have doubt. When we honestly voice our doubt, spiritual
novices sense hospitality. They feel welcome. It's as if you knew they were
going to be at the service—or as if your own doubt helped you understand
theirs.

May the Lord be gracious to us and bless us.

---

3. Fosdick, "The Importance of Doubting Your 'Doubts.'"

Kevin

P.S. Last year our congregation hosted a seminar for folks who welcome refugees to our country. We were struck by the stories of potential immigrants waiting four to five years as their paperwork inched from one desk to the next. And we were struck all over again by the multiple Old Testament instructions to care for the widows and orphans and aliens within our gates. Our guiding text for the weekend was Psalm 113. We sang it and recited it and spoke it. Psalm 113 is a wonderful example of how multifaceted the psalms can be. First used to express the immigrant status of God's own people as outsiders in Egypt, it's recited by Jewish people to begin Passover. Now it could be recited by outsiders on school playgrounds or in board rooms as well as by refugees. It is a timeless gift. I'm sure you can make all of this into a stellar worship frame. May God seat us all with the princes of his people!

July

On Framing Global Mission, Patriotism, and National Holidays

Dear Jordan,

So it's almost the Fourth of July, and you feel like you're in a worship war with "bombs bursting in air."

Did I ever tell you about the Minnesota church where I first became a pastor? I am forever grateful for the warmth and good spirit of those hearty people. They introduced me to small-town living, taught me to dodge the lutefisk served by the local Lutheran church, fostered my love for cross-country skiing (almost a year-round sport there!), and launched me into ministry. The church began nine years before my arrival, and I was their second pastor. It's startling to discover how many habits can develop in such a short time.

Before I arrived, one group in the church donated a set of American and Christian flags. Another group didn't want flags displayed in church. Many in the latter group had adopted children from various countries around the world. While strongly affirming patriotic love for their country, they didn't think national flags belonged in a worship service. Instead, they wanted the worship space to reflect the unity of all Christians expressed in their baptism.

Both groups had significant influence in the church, with members serving on council and in key leadership roles. Unable to come to a consensus on whether the flags should be regularly displayed, the groups learned the flags could travel. One Sunday the flags would be displayed on the main platform with the pulpit and communion table. A few weeks later, folks would find them stored in a basement storage closet. No one knew who moved them. It was as if a militia of muscular church mice were having fun with us. Finally the church council thought it wise to weigh in and forged a compromise: the flags would be permanently displayed in the atrium. But even after the official decree, the flags would still migrate to the front of the sanctuary or sneak back to the closet.

The intersection of patriotism and worship can be a high-voltage subject. In the Christian university where I teach, some students can't carry on a civil discussion on this subject. Two sentences into arguing their perspective, logic fades, emotions rocket, and these kind, sweet, *Christian* students verbally accost all who disagree with them, declaring them unpatriotic miscreant scum and suggesting they move to a country they like better—even if that "country" is Nevada!

Just last month a new member of our congregation said, "I tried to invite my friends back to our church, but they wouldn't return." When pressed about the reason, he answered, "They refuse to go to a church that doesn't have an American flag in front." I'm not sure if Canadians or Brits feel as strongly. A friend from the Dominican Republic says only countries with crosses on their flags should fly them proudly in church.

So how does one frame worship on the weekend of national holiday? A fellow pastor whose congregation brings flags into the worship space for national holidays frames Memorial Day weekend prayers in his church this way:

> Today we remember the high cost of sacrifice. We remember God's sacrifice for us. We remember others' sacrifice for us. And we remember that we are called to live in sacrificial love for each other.

Sometimes a simple statement in a congregational prayer signals (frames) a congregation's honor for their country. On Veteran's Day (Armistice Day) weekend, a leader might say:

> Today we remember and are grateful for all who serve.

Another church addresses this confluence of agendas by displaying the national flags of its members' countries of origin. All hang from the ceiling.

A few years in a row we had mission week in our church. Each time we asked children to carry onto the platform small flags from all thirty-five nations served by our denomination's mission agency. But one year, when the child carrying the United States flag walked onto the platform, a cheer went up. I wondered how the other flag-carriers experienced their non-applause. The following year someone asked me if we could please make the American flag bigger than the others.

One way to frame our calling to honor those in civil authority is to pray on national holidays. Following the earlier example from Mother's Day, we might lead a bidding prayer. A frame might introduce the Bible's call to such prayer:

> The Apostle Paul encourages a young pastor named Timothy to pray for civil leaders: "I urge, then, first of all, that petitions, prayers, intercession, and thanksgiving be made for all people— for kings and all those in authority, that we may live peaceful and quiet lives in all godliness and holiness."[1] Today we're going to mark the Fourth of July by doing exactly that.

We might design a similar frame that highlights our solidarity with Christians of different and varied backgrounds:

> Our friends in the Episcopal and Orthodox churches take the Bible's command to pray for those in authority so seriously that they pray for our congressperson, our governor, and our president every week by name. Today we want to celebrate the holiday by joining our sisters and brothers in prayer.

Or imagine praying for civil leaders with a global flavor, even on a national holiday:

> The Bible urges us to pray for all those in civil authority. Regardless of our political perspective, we know that in a convoluted and ever-changing world like ours, leaders need wisdom. Let's join our fellow believers around the world and pray for our leaders.

Such supportive and honoring prayer might be a special act of faith when the civil leader's ideas and behavior do not match those of the majority of congregants.

What do you think about the possibility of invoking the words of those considered national saints on such weekends? Imagine a frame that says,

> Today, on Presidents Day weekend, we remember what Abraham Lincoln reportedly once told an associate: "I have been driven many times upon my knees by the overwhelming conviction that I had no where else to go." Another time he wrote a Mrs. Lydia Bixby, who had lost five sons in the war between the states, "I pray that our Heavenly Father may assuage the anguish of your bereavement, and leave you only the cherished memory of the loved and lost, and the solemn pride that must be yours to

---

1. 1 Tim 2:1–2, NIV.

have laid so costly a sacrifice upon the altar of freedom."[2] Today we will follow Lincoln's example and turn to God in prayer.

Or what if we pray a prayer written by a national figure like we would pray a prayer offered by Augustine or Mother Teresa or St. Francis? Consider this frame:

> During the most discouraging days of the civil rights movement, Dr. Martin Luther King Jr. said, "To be a Christian without prayer is no more possible than to be alive without breathing."[3] Today let us follow this sentiment and pray for our beloved country.

You might follow such a frame with one of Dr. King's prayers, such as this one:

> Most gracious and all wise God, before whose face the generations rise and fall; Thou in whom we live, and move, and have our being. We thank thee [for] all of thy good and gracious gifts, for life and for health; for food and for raiment; for the beauties of nature and human nature. We come before thee painfully aware of our inadequacies and shortcomings. We realize that we stand surrounded with the mountains of love and we deliberately dwell in the valley of hate. We stand amid the forces of truth and deliberately lie. We are forever offered the high road and yet we choose to travel the low road. For these sins, O God, forgive. Break the spell of that which blinds our minds. Purify our hearts that we may see thee. O God, in these turbulent days when fear and doubt are mounting high, give us broad visions, penetrating eyes, and power of endurance. Help us to work with renewed vigor for a warless world, for a better distribution of wealth, and for a brotherhood that transcends race or color. In the name and spirit of Jesus we pray. Amen.[4]

We might frame a prayer by invoking a saint who fiercely loved his homeland but who indisputably belonged to people (the church) of every nation:

> Today on this national holiday, we follow the example of a wise Christian writing at the time of the first apostles. In a letter to his friend Diognetus, a pagan trying to understand this new thing

2. Lincoln, "Letter to Mrs. Bixby."

3. The source of this quote is unknown; it has been attributed in equal measure to King and to Martin Luther.

4. King, "Prayers," 137.

called "Christianity," this new believer wrote words that get to the heart of a Christian's relationship with their country: they "dwell in their own countries, but simply as sojourners." He goes on, accenting that Jesus is the center of all our belonging. He described Jesus followers as those for whom "every foreign land is . . . their native country, and every land of their birth . . . a land of strangers."[5] In this spirit, let us pray for the country we love.

I wonder if the centurion whose servant Jesus healed (Matt 8:5–13) or the other who declared at Jesus' death, "Surely this man was the Son of God!" (Mark 15:39) ever thought about this?[6]

Yours,
Kevin

On Psalms as Spiritual (and Ecclesial) Biography

Dear Jordan,

Your words are inspiring. It's more than just accurate to connect the psalms to the puzzling tangle of human emotions; it's deeply wise. It's to be a doctor of souls. To create a frame like you did, giving voice to the deepest doubts and anxiety of all attendees, helps spiritual novices find their way inside the faith. So often folks from the outside assume that people of faith have it all together—and that having it all together is a prerequisite for attending worship. But the Psalter shows us we worship in utter honesty, even chaos. Did you know your frame connects to an idea of Athanasius taken up by John Calvin, who called the psalms the "anatomy of the soul"?

Last year a friend lost her husband suddenly. She's a woman of deep faith. But it's all she can do to carry on. And that's after a year of grieving. If a church sings or models only spiritual enthusiasm embodied in upbeat worship, she won't find her voice or a way to lament in church. Authentic faith is always mixed with doubt and disarray. So yes, I love how you named these realities in your frame.

What do you think of connecting the full range of human experience and emotions to personal faith stories as a further way for people to see the church is big enough to hold the full range of their emotions?

5. Mathetes, "Epistle of Mathetes to Diognetus," V.

6. For more on the confluence of baptism and national identity, and to wonder at the reality that people of every country can be spiritual insiders, see my article "Scythian Worship?"

This weekend we celebrate Martin Luther King Jr.'s birthday. In the darkest days of the civil rights movement, when many of his fellow Christians mocked and vilified his work, when fellow Christians spit on and bullied and threatened him and his followers, Dr. King and his close friend Ralph Abernathy found comfort in Psalm 27, even while they were in prison. Let's pray that psalm now.

Sometimes setting the psalm into a story from another part of the Christian church can show our solidarity and willingness to learn from them:

Thomas Merton lost both his mother and father by the time he was sixteen years old. First a nominal Anglican, then an atheist, and always a social activist, Merton later became a Trappist monk, giving voice to the spiritual yearnings of a generation. He once said, "Nowhere can we be more certain that we are praying with the Holy Spirit than when we pray the Psalms."[7] Imagine that: God gives us the psalms so we have words to pray back to God.

Or make it especially personal, both for you as worship leaders and for the congregation:

Every funeral I've ever led has included the familiar words of Psalm 23. They voice our hope in the midst of life's darkest shadows. Maybe as we pray these words you'll imagine them said at your own funeral. Maybe you'll think of someone you love who has passed away. We invite you to acknowledge your grief, and lean on the One who gives comfort.

The psalms, the most original worship elements of all, come to us with built-in complexity. Rather than sweeping that complexity under the rug, or hiding it in embarrassment, why not use it as a way to invite people more deeply inside the faith?

In all life's doubt and wonder,
Kevin

---

7. Merton, *Praying the Psalms*, 18.

On Biographies of Church Outsiders (Hearing A Culture's Own Poets)

Dear Jordan,

I'm glad you all like the idea of biography as a frame. We live in a world of stories. People delight in telling stories, hearing stories, and watching stories. I'm always amazed at how often children (and the inner child that still lives in the body of senior citizens) can tell or watch the same story for the hundredth time with equal enthusiasm. It's no wonder that so much of the Bible is story.

Since the Bible tells the one true story, and since worship enacts the one true story, it can be helpful to highlight and employ its nature as story. So often theologians and pastors and worship leaders have stripped the story from much-loved doctrine, often in the name of truth. Why not instead help worshipers see how the stories they hear each day connect to or disconnect from the gospel story? Doesn't the Apostle Paul do this when he says "one of Crete's own prophets has said . . ."?[8] In the same way, Paul quoted Athenian philosophy and religion back to the Greeks, saying, "As I walked around and looked carefully at your objects of worship, I even found an altar with this inscription: to an unknown god."[9] We might say in both instances that Paul tells the true gospel story using a frame from the local cultural story.

It can be tempting in worship to let your disagreement with people show. Often this happens unconsciously. It can come across as being disagreeable, a kind of against-ness toward the very people we're trying to invite into a gospel conversation. Instead, what if worship leaders show an astute (and fair) understanding of local philosophy? Like the mission-oriented apostle, we could use that understanding to highlight the grace of God's true story.

What about a frame that quotes people's philosophy back to them? I told you about the wonderful English/philosophy major on our team. She formed a frame in this way:

> Decades ago, Franz Kafka said that contemporary people laugh at the idea of guilt but still carry a nagging sense that something is wrong with us. We each have an inner voice in our own heart calling us an idiot, or a fool, or a failure. Is that why we can't take criticism? Is that why some of us kill ourselves with work, numb ourselves with drink, or don't eat at all? We know something

8. Titus 1:12, NIV.
9. Acts 17:23, NIV.

is wrong with us. Let's now participate in the classic Christian worship way of dealing with that reality.

Her frame set us up to participate in a prayer of confession and words of assurance in a culturally relevant way. Imagine this variation, based on a timeless movie that many adults and children have seen:

> In the original classic Disney movie *The Lion King*, James Earl Jones gives voice to Mufasa, the majestic king of the African animals. Teaching his son, Simba, to act like a true king, Mufasa says something stirring and unforgettable. He tells Simba, "Remember who you are." As we remember our baptism this morning, we want to hear God's voice reminding us that we are God's children, spiritual sons and daughters, called to live as divine royalty.

Or imagine using a local or global news source to voice a current issue. Suppose a worship leader says at some point in late August or early September:

> These days, in an annual ritual, thousands of students are leaving home for college. Many students from our own congregation are part of the trek. In a recent *New York Times* essay, Kerry Corrigan wondered about such children leaving home for college: "What if they remember only the worst parts? What version of us [parents] will they be taking with them?"[10] What if our children, our friends, our neighbors only remember our foibles and fumbles, our weaknesses and shortcomings? What if that's all God sees? Thank God for grace. Thank God for his promise that, in Jesus, the version of us he sees is framed by the redeeming work of Jesus on the cross.

This is another place it helps to know your congregation well. Quoting a certain news feed or media network may be a trigger for people in your congregation, sending all sorts of signals, intended or not, about who belongs and who doesn't in your congregation. So might a reference to college attendance. And you know best if the underlying guilt or neurosis behind Corrigan's questions resonates in your neighborhood.

So I offer this humbly, but I hope it might stir possibilities. The idea is not, as you surmise, to appear to be a hip and relevant Christian. It's to encourage you as a physician of souls. You know the particular ailments and remedies and what speaks most deeply to your congregation and neighbors.

10. Corrigan, "Advice to My College Freshman."

Karl Barth, arguably the most noted theologian of his generation, once said: "Take your Bible and take your newspaper, and read both. But interpret newspapers from your Bible."[11] The gospel story both connects to and disconnects from a nation's and a city's story. What if wise worship leaders use that for framing worship?

Your fellow student of culture,
Kevin

On Passing the Peace in Your (and Every) Neighborhood[12]

Dear Jordan,

After our worship service last week, one of our staff—the delightful Peruvian woman I've mentioned before who greets everyone (first-time attendees and dearly loved regulars) with a warm South American hug—got handed a note. Here's what it said:

> Dear Friends,
>
> On Sunday during the passing of the peace, we wonder: *How* do we pass the peace? What do we say? What do we need to do?
>
> May I suggest that giving a verbal example would be helpful? Maybe modeling something like, "The peace of the Lord be with you," and in reply, "And also with you."
>
> Your thoughts and ideas are appreciated on how to explain what to do and say in the passing of the peace. Thanks! And God bless you!

The note won points for its congeniality. You might even say the note on passing the peace was itself a kind of passing the peace. (Sorry, I couldn't resist.)

As with many of the classic service elements, we needed to retrofit our worship service to include passing the peace. For twenty years we simply introduced this moment in the service as our "meet and greet" time. There was efficiency to it: we needed to send students to age-appropriate classes, and the extended greeting time gave parents a moment to walk their children to classes or to take a quick bathroom break. If there was going to be a noisy interlude anyway, why not leverage it as a moment to make personal connections and to let the ushers and greeters work their hospitality magic?

11. "Barth in Retirement."

12. The material in this letter (adapted) first appeared in my July 30, 2018, *Reformed Worship* blog post "The Gospel in a Handshake."

But eventually we reconsidered. We were increasing the frequency of Eucharist; why not reconsider the eucharistic elements as well? Why merely shake hands when you can pass God's peace?

More than a chance to simply stretch our legs or get our blood flowing so we can better endure sitting through a sermon, the passing of the peace was placed in the liturgy of the early church for wise theological reasons. It's a way to concretely live the Sermon on the Mount. We extend forgiveness and grace to members of the body of Christ right around us.

In the third century, Eastern Orthodox congregations had one of the deacons call aloud at this point in the service, "Is there any man that keepeth aught against his fellow?"[13]

Can you imagine? If you try it in your worship service, let me know. I'd like to hear how that goes! The passing of the peace is a way to live the practical wisdom of the Bible: "Whoever does not love their brother and sister, whom they have seen, cannot love God, whom they have not seen."[14]

It's both ordinary and breathtaking. Imagine a married couple fighting on the way to church, arguing in the car or as they walk.[15] Most of the time they're not really arguing about what they're arguing about. They're not really angry about a forgotten date on the calendar or about a bookkeeping disagreement or yet another meal of leftovers. They're actually giving voice to their anxiety about their children's well-being in an increasingly unsafe world, or the haunting fear that their wedding day dreams are indiscernibly fading into the same tedium they regularly witness in the dreary reality of their aging parents. So, they grumble about a curt remark from yesterday or a look from this morning. And then they come to church. And someone like you or your team invites them, in a wise ancient practice, to pass each other the peace of Christ. These squabbling married people say to each other, "The peace of Christ be with you." And they learn to respond, "And also with you."

The peace of Christ be with you!
Kevin

---

13. Anonymous church fathers, *Didascalia Apostolorum*, VII.ii.54.

14. 1 John 4:20, NIV.

15. Warren, *Liturgy of the Ordinary*, 78–80.

On Passing the Peace as the Gospel in a Handshake

Dear Jordan,

I'm delighted your team immediately captured the simple wonder of passing the peace. In our church we've come to describe it as "the gospel in a handshake."

Two Sundays ago I was sitting in front of a grade-school brother and sister. Their parents were leading our congregation in singing, and the siblings sat side by side. Fully participating, they sang. They confessed their sins. They remembered their baptism. Side by side, with fellow congregants of multiple generations. And then came this moment. A worship leader simply framed the idea and then invited everyone to pass the peace. They turned toward each other, brother and sister, rivals and friends, foes and equals, comrades and competitors, with the thousand things that define their relationship and push and pull them apart. It was so simple. And wonderful. They did as they were invited. They turned to face each other, shook hands, and said, "The peace of Christ be with you," followed by, "And also with you." Then each, in their gregarious grade-school ways, turned to shake my hand and say the same to me. I wonder if they noticed I was misty-eyed. I had just beheld a mystery. A living embodiment of grace. The gospel in a handshake.

I found myself wondering what this practice might create in these two over a lifetime of worship? An ability to have civil conversations with political rivals? A marriage that can last decades? A flourishing relationship with siblings and parents? An ability to cooperate collegially with work colleagues and competitors? To echo Schmemann, passing the peace is another way worship enables us to become our true selves.

You asked how we frame such a gift. Often simply, as recommended by our wonderful staff person's note we discussed earlier:

> In daily life, we greet each other by shaking hands and saying, "Good morning." Here in church we do that in a special way. We pass the peace of Christ. One person turns to you and says, "The peace of Christ be with you," and the other responds, "And also with you." We invite you to do that now.

This thin frame may be as simple as it gets. But other times we want to remember the whole gospel in a handshake. After all, the peace of Christ is not a cheap peace. It's not a cover-up of conflicts. It's not simply being nice or papering over wrongs. It's not the denial of deep hurt, the simple solution for conflict avoiders. No, it's the deep longing of every human heart. When we pass the peace, we show solidarity with refugees from Syria and brothers and sisters in underground congregations in Asia or in churches that meet on Hawaiian beaches—all sorts of churches around the world. So why not frame it that way?

> We all live with a deep longing for the entire world to flourish. We want every child on every continent to live in safety, to play without fear, and to daydream with hope about their future. We long for the day when God will bring his all-consuming peace. The Bible calls that *shalom*. Today we invite you to show solidarity with God's redeeming work around the world with a simple greeting. Turn to someone nearby and say, "The peace of Christ be with you."

I suspect you're thinking I might be overenthused about such a simple act. But it's hard to overstate how in this simple act God extends us God's love and mercy, and we move toward a time when the oppressed are set free.

If you think I'm enthused about passing the peace, you should have been in our congregation yesterday when Kyu, our seminary intern, introduced it. His enthusiasm for God's love and grace is boundless. So it didn't really surprise any of us when he got so worked up about passing the peace. Here's what he said:

> Friends, the church of all times and places has been participating in this ancient practice of passing the peace. How we do this is pretty simple. We turn to a neighbor around us and look into their eyes. Then we extend handshakes or hugs.
>
> Now the meaning of this is even cooler. As we extend the peace, we are identifying ourselves with Christ, who by his own death brings peace and joy into the world, making peace with humanity—you and me. We are really saying, "There is brokenness in this world." Sometimes we feel deeply that life is difficult, and we get discouraged. But be *confident* [he emphasized this word with marked enthusiasm] that Christ has brought his peace, and it is with us. So let us turn to one another and with joy and confidence say "The peace of Christ be with you," and so pass the peace.[16]

I hope that gets you started.
Forever and always: the peace of Christ be with you,
Kevin

---

16. Thanks to Kyu Hahn for letting me share this and for his boundless enthusiasm for passing the peace during worship.

On Passing the Peace During Trouble

Dear Jordan,

I know. I wish you could have been there too. You have to know how much our congregation loves Kyu. We all knew his frame was a bit long. But no one seemed to mind. We were swept up in his contagious desire for everyone to experience shalom and for enemies to become friends.

In one way, this practice is a kind of prayer. We are praying that Christ would be our peace. After all, we don't make it; we receive it. That reminds me of how my friend Neal introduced this practice. In his thoughtful way, he said:

> All through his ministry Jesus encountered storms: storms of anxiety and relational chaos or scary winds and waves. Each time, he said one word that brought healing and calm: "Peace." Today each of us is experiencing a kind of storm inside. In the face of such storms, and because of Jesus, would you turn to one another and say "Peace. The peace of Christ be with you."[17]

I hope you found that moving; I was overwhelmed when I heard it. How did he know? How did he know that just then I needed to experience the whole gospel in a handshake? Imagine saying that when your congregation has evacuees fleeing a fire, or immigrants still unsettled in a new city, or parents trying to keep their children safe on a violent street or an ordinary school playground.

On certain weeks there is nothing more essential for a church than to embody this worship treasure. A few months ago, after someone in another state walked onto a high school campus and began a shooting rampage, killing dozens of teenagers and staff, a worship team member used this frame to invite us to pass the peace:

> Friends, we learned again this week that the world is not the way it's supposed to be. This weekend we had a seminar and learned about refugees who live in United Nations camps for years with little hope of getting free. This week a gunman walked into a Florida school and started shooting. That's not the way it's supposed to be. Students are supposed to worry about algebra and grammar, not bullets. Teachers are supposed to worry about lesson plans and after-school events, not gunmen terrorizing their hallways.
>
> The Bible promises us a day is coming. It will be a day when things *are* the way they're supposed to be. Gunmen will no

17. Adams, "Shaping a Congregation's Worship DNA."

longer threaten students and teachers. Refugees will no longer rot in forgotten camps. On that day, the peace of God will cover the cosmos. In longing for that day, in hope for that day, in a pledge to speed that day, let us do what Christians have done for centuries and say to each other, "The peace of Christ be with you."[18]

As you can imagine, we could hardly dare speak after such a frame. To pass the peace that morning was to do something brave and holy. We all felt a stab of grief—and grace. And then we passed the peace as if our lives depended on it.

Perhaps passing the peace can seem a quaint, overly simplistic relic from a bygone era. And often, the actual practice of passing the peace is ironically chaotic. People wander far from their seats or make impromptu adaptations of the practice, turning to each other and asking, "What's up?" Some make awkward comments; others stand in self-conscious silence. But at other times, in the week of a school shooting or a seminar on welcoming refugees, it embodies the entire gospel. It truly is "the gospel in a handshake." I do hope you try it. Let me know how it goes.

The peace of Christ be with you,
Kevin

---

18. Matt Timms, Granite Springs Church liturgy, February 18, 2018.

August

On Collecting Money: Framing the Offering

Dear Jordan,

Your video clip brought tears to my eyes. Yes, tears of laughter. But also the tears of knowing, of having experienced firsthand the kind of up-front fumbling it illustrates. I'm cheered by the humility of its main actor. That your seminary intern can laugh at herself will be a gift to her and all in ministry with her. Your group is wise not to post this on social media, but I was delighted to see it. Anyone who has ever led worship, let alone delivered a worship frame, salutes her. Somehow it is funnier that it all happened as she introduced the offering! And then one of the ushers didn't show up, so she actually had to step in and *collect* the offering too? Priceless.

You likely know, and have heard over the years, a version of an offering worship frame with an emphasis on making room for folks sometimes called "spiritual seekers." It's a frequently used frame:

> We are delighted you are here this morning. If this is your first
> time in a worship service in many years, or your first time ever,
> we want you to know that the offering is not for you. While you
> are welcome to participate, please don't feel obligated.

This frame has become common in many places, even with folks who are not conscious of how such words really serve as a worship frame. For years we said something much like that. It works well.

You can also go the opposite way with an offering frame. Rather than saying, "Please don't feel obligated," why not challenge folks to be astonishingly generous? An offering frame can offer a clear vision for why giving is worship.

> This time of offering is a call for all who call our church their
> spiritual home. As individuals, most of us can't influence a
> neighborhood or renew a city, but by being generous together

we can do amazing things. May our giving today reflect our worship.

Lately we've most often focused the orientation of our offering frame to focus on God as the giver. Often we keep the offering frame thin and simply say something like:

> God is generous with us. In this part of the service, the offering, we invite you to respond in generosity yourself.

As I said, that frame is short and to the point. Other Sundays we do a slight variation that is a bit thicker. It is framed in the spirit of a collect, a prayer that names and celebrates one of God's virtues and then invites us to live it:

> God is generous with us. Every day he gives us gifts of which we are conscious or unconscious: friends, family, daily bread, opportunities to serve according to our gifts, and work. In this next part of the service, we are all invited to respond to God's generosity by being generous ourselves. In doing so we join generous Christians around the world and through all history who selflessly give to enable their neighborhoods to flourish.

As you can see, the frame revels in God's unending generosity and summons us to be big-hearted in response. At Christmas, we often do a seasonal variation:

> In the Spirit of the Magi who brought their gifts to Jesus so long ago, we invite you to also give an offering to the Babe of Bethlehem.

As always, I'm very curious what your group will design on their own. And I'm sure you'll all give your seminarian another chance. Maybe we could show her solidarity by sending her videos of our own blunders!

Yours,
Kevin

On Framing Sermons (Often toward Eucharist)

Dear Jordan,

You're entirely right. Sermons can profoundly benefit from framing or wayfinding. A wise preacher carefully designs frames within a sermon, acknowledging listeners come from an astonishing diversity of spiritual places. Preaching at Easter, for instance, a thoughtful pastor might say, "For some of us the resurrection is a given, something we've built our life upon. For others here it seems a contradiction to every verifiable medical test ever conducted. People do not rise again after three days."

Or preaching through an Old Testament passage, a speaker can glibly gloss over violence, and deaths seem a given. Not every sermon can thoroughly address the violence present in a text, but even a simple statement such as "This seems profoundly violent to us, people from another time and era" can at least show a pastor acknowledges and respects people of differing faith perspectives.

A few years ago I walked out of a church gathering and into the parking lot with several college-aged people who had been attending our church. As the group dispersed I noticed a bumper sticker on the back of a young woman's car. It announced, "April 1: Atheists' Day," complete with a Bible proof text underneath. I was dismayed. Having always experienced her as a winsome, bubbly, gregarious person, I wasn't prepared for this exhibit of her faith. In fact, we had just had a small-group conversation about contagious faith! How did that bumper sticker start a conversation with a secular person?

If only we as worship leaders and preachers didn't unconsciously do the same thing. If we had a dollar for every time we heard a throwaway line from a preacher that needlessly excluded spiritual explorers, we could buy you every worship book ever written. Phrases that proclaim, "We all know . . ." or state, "You all remember the Old Testament story of . . ." or declare, "We Christians teach . . ." assume every listener is a spiritual insider.

One way to frame a sermon, as we've been saying, is inside the sermon itself. Another is before the sermon with what is historically called the Prayer of Enlightenment, which can name the variety of faith experiences in the room:

> Father, we are a tangled variety of people today. Some of us come with joy, so grateful to be here. Others bring only dismay, suffocating from doubt and loss. Still others are exhausted, weary by our own internal demands and those of others. And now we open the Bible. Speak your good news to us. Let it be for us your words of life.

A vintage prayer from the Church of Scotland shows these same qualities:

> Blessed Lord,
> who caused all holy Scriptures to be written for our learning:
> Grant us so to hear them,
> read, mark, learn, and inwardly digest them,
> that we may embrace and ever hold fast

the blessed hope of everlasting life,
which you have given us in our Savior Jesus Christ. Amen.[1]

Another move a preacher can make is to arrange the end of the sermon to frame the Eucharist that often follows. Suppose a sermon is on Acts 9, the dramatic conversion story of the Apostle Paul. What if a preacher ends like this:

> In a few moments we are going to invite you to come forward to the table of the Lord. To get in line and come forward is to say, "I need converting too." It is to say, "This is my Damascus road." It is to join a community, the church, filled with people least likely to believe.

One gift you can give your congregation is to have a joint sense of framing among all who plan and lead any part of a worship service or church life. By assuming non-believers are present in every aspect of ministry (except maybe the deacon or elder team!), you create an unmistakable sense that they are fully welcome with all their doubts and questions and disbelief.

Grateful to be together on the Damascus road,
Kevin

On Praying the Prayer Jesus Taught

Dear Jordan,

Right. Here again the task—to teach people to pray—seems beyond words. Somehow we try to express with words what no words can express.

Thankfully, as you know, Jesus' disciples needed to learn, too. We often refer to their question when introducing the answer, this most famous of prayers. Here again, we think a few words are better than many. The simplest frame might go like this:

> Together let's pray the words that Jesus taught his disciples.

We often say a slightly expanded invitation:

> None of us is an expert at prayer. We don't know what to pray, or where to start. Neither did Jesus' disciples. So one day they asked Jesus to teach them, and since that day generations have prayed the words Jesus gave. Let's pray them together.

Or another simple frame:

1. *The Book of Common Prayer*, Year A, Proper 28.

> In the next few moments we're going to invite you to pray very
> likely the most often repeated words in human history, words
> Jesus gave to his followers to pray back to him. Let's pray Jesus'
> own words.

This, of course, is another opportunity to acknowledge and accent our solidarity with Christians around the world. Sometimes we voice that unity by
acknowledging the prayer's two historic names familiar to people of Catholic, Orthodox, and Protestant families:

> In the next few moments we will pray together words prayed
> millions of times already today by our sisters and brothers
> around the world. Some call it the Lord's Prayer. Some call it the
> Our Father. Whatever you call it, we invite you to join Chris-
> tians around the world, in cathedrals and huts, gathered on
> beachfronts and hiding in caves, rich and poor, sick and healthy,
> free or imprisoned. Let's pray words that unite us to God and to
> each other.

Do you see again the formative power of using these oft-used elements in worship? They deeply unite us to the worldwide church. There's
nothing sensational or titillating about praying what is so familiar. Some
might critique praying them each week as an empty or near-empty ritual. It's
true some participants recite the words halfheartedly, or are distracted by
a toddler's fidgeting, their inner anxiety, or the cell phone buzzing in their
pocket. But in praying these words week after week, we voice our place in
the worldwide church. I suspect that by now I'm preaching to the choir, but
I can't resist. In worshiping via these ancient practices, our personal stories
and encounters with Jesus are wrapped up in the story of all believers into
God's eternal story.

Yours,
Kevin

On Eucharist: Welcoming Spiritual Novices

Dear Jordan,

I loved your Eucharist story! As I read your letter I could picture it clearly.
After so many months of sitting in his seat, Funjab came forward, waiting in
the line of people walking forward to receive communion. Then he received
the elements with open hands, taking in the words, "The body of Christ for

you." It's such a thrill when people who've been waiting in the wings come forward to participate and to receive grace.

I'm also sympathetic to your question about his wife, Sanjab. It's so well phrased: "How do we both invite people to participate in the moment of communion and show hospitality to those who do not?"

What if I describe a couple of the invitations we give, and describe how we frame Eucharist, then let you and your team see what is best for your context and tradition? One of our long-standing invitations is more explanation than framing. We say,

> We are now at that point in the service that we sometimes call Eucharist. The word *Eucharist* comes from a beautiful Greek word that means "thanks." And indeed, when we participate, we are thankful that Jesus has done everything that needed to be done for us to participate. Sometimes we call it "communion" because in this act we commune with the Father, Son, and Holy Spirit. And we commune with each other, as sisters and brothers in this congregation, and with sisters and brothers in congregations all over the world, in huts and homes and cathedrals and prisons. And sometimes we call this the Lord's Supper. Jesus himself is the host of this meal. He gives himself to us through his death and resurrection. And in an overwhelming moment of hospitality, he invites us forward to participate.

As I said, it's a bit long, and more of an explanation than a frame. But we use it regularly because, like you, we have so many people attend who do not have any church memory or experience, and they appreciate such guidance.

Sometimes, on the other end of complexity, we simply say:

> We are going to celebrate the saving work of Jesus. On the way
> to that celebration, would you join in this ancient conversation?

I find the moment of actual participation, as people come forward to receive the sacrament, a moment of unending grace. Forward they come. Some sashay or parade. Others amble or saunter or stroll. Some hobble, assisted by wheelchairs or walkers or crutches. Some look hopeful or peaceful; others are racked with pain. Each week people stagger forward. It's a kind of holy mess. Behold, the body of Christ.

Each congregation has its own voice, a word of truth and grace about who is welcome and a word of pastoral wisdom about who should wait and who should participate. How we communicate this holy invitation or give direction on non-participation is one of the most arduous pastoral and hospitality moves. In our congregation we err on the side of inclusion and invitation. Each week we acknowledge, in words or print, that some present will not be ready to participate. We tend to leave that to an individual's own discretion. Other communities make it clear: this meal is for all *baptized* Christians or all *catholic* Christians or all *orthodox* believers. Even when the table is fenced, a word of inclusive framing can be helpful:

> We invite all baptized Christians [or everyone here] to come
> forward and participate in this family meal of Christians. If you
> are not yet baptized [or not yet a follower of Jesus], we invite you
> to come forward to receive a blessing.

Again, our congregation chooses to err on the side of invitation. Maybe that's because we see communion as a means of grace to people in all stages of their spiritual journey.

Through the years several of our attendees have told us, "I became a Christian while taking communion." Theologically that's messy, but in our context, worship is always a bit messy. When we offer the bread and wine we encourage participants to respond by saying "Thanks be to God." But in our informal California context, people respond with all kinds of declarations: "Happy Sunday, Kevin!" or "Thanks for that wonderful sermon!" or "Nice weather, eh?" When a man with dementia came to receive a few months ago, he paused, looked deep into my eyes, and said, "You were on fire today with that sermon, Rev." Hearing his commentary, the next participant said to me at half volume, "His wife sure has her hands full with him, doesn't she!"

Several weeks ago, a fairly new attendee told me, "This is my first time taking communion; I'm so happy I could burst. I wanted to share this with you."

All this may be a bit off script, but it's also a cause for joy and celebration. How do you invite folks like your friends Funjab and Sanjab to receive grace whether or not they participate?

Maybe one word of wisdom is to frame the invitation by quoting those who have gone before. In our tradition, one way we frame an invitation to participate in the sacrament is to say, before the communion liturgy itself, words from one of our favorite historic confessions, the Heidelberg Catechism:

> We now invite everyone forward to participate in Eucharist. All
> who are truly displeased with their sins, who trust they are for-
> given and that their remaining weakness is covered by Jesus' suf-
> fering and death, and who desire more and more to strengthen

and amend their life of Jesus-following are invited to come to the table.[2]

Framing the invitation with a 500-year-old document does assure people that you aren't being fast or loose or novel with your invitation.

God bless and increase the number of all those who come forward and those waiting in the wings.

Kevin

On Communion (or On Communing—or Not)

Dear Jordan,

I know. I see the irony too. Or, we might say, the frustration. The sacraments are gifts given to make the gospel clear. But instead they often display how different traditions of Christians are clearly *not* in full communion. I'm very sympathetic to Henri Nouwen, the Dutch Roman Catholic priest and much-loved writer on spiritual formation, who rather than directly defying his Catholic hierarchy simply invited people present to participate in the Eucharist. I'm not saying his is the only path forward, but it does model communion as *communion*.

I grew up with a somber, introspective (even brooding at times) pattern of communion. We received communion only four times a year, and each time was marked by melancholy music and a framing—in a form read with little expression from the back of the hymnal—in a minor key. What a contrast to the free-flowing Eucharist invitation of Nouwen, who spoke the entire liturgy from memory! Those who participated as congregants and retreatants and guests remember Nouwen's uninhibited freedom in leading communion. Wildly and enthusiastically, he gestured a welcome that echoed and accented his welcoming words.

As we've experienced in our congregation, and as you have also relayed about yours, the Lord's Supper can be, by design or accident, an experience that converts. By nature, grace is surprising—a mystery beyond categories and formulas. A middle-aged dad attended our congregation for several years. He told me this was his first experience going to church, and he found it life-giving and life-altering. He said it took him more than a year to come to faith. When I asked if there was a moment when he *knew* he was on the inside of belief, he responded without hesitation, "It was a few months ago when I first participated in communion. At the moment I ate and drank, I believed."

2. Adapted from the Heidelberg Catechism, Q&A 81.

I responded kindly, nodded my head, and said something reflective about the curious and amazing ways of God. But I remember thinking, "That's not how we scripted the steps of conversion in seminary." Or in our prescribed worship forms and formulas. We taught that one ought first to be baptized and only then participate in communion. But here (again) was a dazzling display of God's creative grace.

If communion is explained (framed) well, an unbeliever will have a specific and visible way to see her current spiritual state. She'll see there's a marked difference between living for oneself and walking with Jesus in discipleship. Framed well, the Lord's Supper confronts each of us with the questions "Are you in communion with God today?" and "Would you like to receive God's grace now?" In this way, the means of grace can be an effective way to help a person to do a spiritual inventory. We can imagine spiritual seekers coming to realize they are not Christians during the fencing of the table. How do you frame that?

I'll be curious to hear your response.
Kevin

On Altar Calls and Eucharist

Dear Jordan,

I read with interest your question: "Should you include an altar call in your worship service? And if so, how?" From our previous conversation, I know you won't likely be satisfied with my answer, but again I say, "It depends." I have several friends who are pastors in the Baptist tradition. They tell me, "If I went a week without an altar call, I'd be looking for a new place to work!"

Last week I read an article[3] by a much-loved college chaplain. He was walking across campus when a student stopped him to ask, "Why don't you offer an altar call every week?"

He said her question, asked so earnestly, "dug me like an elbow in the ribs." With her sweet and innocent demeanor, was she accusing him of neglecting part of his pastoral duty? Let me share some of his thoughts, and his answer:

> "Why don't we have an altar call every week?" Her question hung in the air like bait. I wasn't sure how to get into all of this on the sidewalk. And so, rather than explaining the inherent theological trouble, rather than pointing out that she is arguably semi-Pelagian (students look at me funny when I talk that way),

3. Johnson, "The Altar Call of Hope."

I responded by simply saying, "We do have an altar call. Every week."

She looked confused. "When?"

"Every week I invite Hope to come to the Lord's Table."

She tilted her head sideways and furrowed her eyebrows into a question mark. I could tell she didn't get the connection. I went on to explain that the invitation to the sacrament is a kind of altar call.

"Hmm . . . I hadn't thought of it like that," she said.

Every week on Hope College's campus, our Sunday evening service, The Gathering, culminates with the celebration of the Lord's Supper. Every week we pray together The Great Thanksgiving. Every week we lift up our hearts "because it is holy and right to do so." Every week we proclaim the mystery of the faith: "Christ has died, Christ is risen, Christ will come again!" Every week we gather together at the table and "remember the perfect sacrifice offered once on the cross by our Lord Jesus Christ for the sin of the whole world." Every week we bid the Holy Spirit to bless this bread and this cup "so that we may grow up into Christ Jesus our Lord." And every week I offer an invitation to the gathered community to respond to God's love in Jesus Christ by coming forward to what I like to call "the Table of Hope."

Reading this brought to mind Eucharist at our church. It never gets old. And it might, as the chaplain said, "be the best part of my week." Forward they come. Some glide; others mosey or amble. Some shuffle, assisted by walkers or hobbling on crutches. Some look expectant or serene; others obviously have discomfort. As I've said, it's a kind of holy mess. Behold, the body of Christ.

Our eucharistic invitation is also a kind of altar call. Always. One frame we use goes like this:

On the cross Jesus said, "It is finished."

In that one word, he made it clear that everything that needs to be done for your salvation has already been done by him. You simply need to come forward, with hands extended to receive his grace. To participate in this Christian meal is to say, "I accept what Jesus has done for me." We invite you forward, even for the first time, to receive his grace.

It's a wonder. Each week people new and old, familiar and unfamiliar, healthy and wounded, walk forward to participate in a taste of heaven. Sometimes I extend the above frame with an additional, personal paragraph:

My great-grandmother was a devout woman. She attended worship multiple times each week. She was generous to the poor, faithful in prayer, and raised her children to follow Jesus in joy. But she never took communion. When her children asked why, she said, "Because I'm not good enough."

And of course, with all due respect to my great-grandmother, she wasn't. And neither are you. And neither am I. But that's not the point. The point is that Jesus said, "*Tetelestai*" (It is finished). *He* is good enough. And all we need to participate in communion is *his* goodness. Would you come forward to receive it?

It's like framing a miracle. Each week we invite attendees to take their place at the table freely set for them to commune with the invisible and visible redeemed of every tribe and language and people and nation and generation. Even my great-grandmother.

Yours in grace,
Kevin

On Giving and Receiving Blessings

Dear Jordan,

How do you end a worship service? It's not a simple question, is it?

In the first days of our congregation (okay, in the first *years* of our congregation) we ended services with a more pious version of "See you all later." As you now know, some of our attendees, with a church background in a certain slice of evangelicalism, wanted us to end each week with an altar call—to invite people to pray a prayer that invites Jesus into their heart. I'm sympathetic. If a worship service leads a person from interest in faith to commitment, why not guide them along the way?

Even in those early days, I found myself craving something more. But I wasn't convinced that ending the service with a come-to-Jesus moment was what we wanted either—at least not every week. So eventually, as with other worship elements, we looked back to the beginning for our ending.

It's no wonder the historic church service ends worship with a blessing. Who doesn't want to experience the smiling face of God's loving approval? Don't we spend most of our lives working or earning or esteeming our way to get a blessing, even as it seems to elude us?

Like everything that happens before it, the blessing can seem strange. In our tradition, the pastor often raises her hands to symbolize the moment of blessing. Even this simple gesture can seem awkward. How often and where in life do people raise their hands over us in blessing?

A pastor from another church said his custom was to offer the blessing with one hand that he held straight and outward from his body. He thought one hand made the moment more intimate and unassuming. But when his next-door neighbor attended his congregation as a guest, he got unexpected and alarming feedback. "The service was all fine," reported his friend. "But why do you raise your hand in that somewhat Nazi salute at the end of the service? That really surprised me. Why do you do it?"

I won't give you suggestions on the exact way to raise your hands except to say, given that story, maybe two hands are better than one. But I do want to answer your question: "How do you frame the final blessing?" Let me offer several suggestions, again knowing you may find them directly helpful or use them to develop something more appropriate for your context. Here are some ways we frame the blessing. See what you think:

> All through this service you've received God's grace: grace in the music, grace in our praying and liturgy, grace (we hope, knowing this is often the weakest link) in the sermon, and grace in communion. Now God gets the last word, and it's one of grace. Would you receive his grace?

Or here's a frame we like that states the same idea more simply:

> In worship, we believe God gets the first word and the last word. We began the service receiving his opening word of grace; now we end with his last word before we are sent.

Or another version:

> Of all the things God might say to us as we go from here, imagine this: that because of Jesus' life and work, he sends us out with his approving love.

Sometimes, as you know, we like to frame worship elements with a nod to their use in the church of all times and places. And it's not just because some people really feel like they've been to church when we quote an old language. To give the final blessing with this historic framework, we sometimes say:

> An ancient Latin Mass ended with these simple words: *Ite, missa est*. It means "Go, you are sent." God has given us his grace in the music, in the liturgy, in the sermon, and in the Eucharist. He now sends you out with a blessing so that you can be a blessing this week. Would you receive it?

To accent the sending without the Latin, and when the theme of our service especially accents the brokenness of our world or the depths of human foibles and misdirection or woundedness, we sometimes say,

> Our world is thirsty for people of good news. You've received good news; you've been called and equipped to embody it. Would you receive a blessing so we can be people of good news in a world desperate for grace?

I'll be curious to hear which of these you think might work best in your context, or to hear what your team is creating for your setting.

Blessings,
Kevin

On Special Blessings, Inside or Outside a Worship Service

Dear Jordan,

You want to talk more about blessings? No apology is needed. Who doesn't?

Sometimes on special occasions we act out our closing blessing by reciting from the psalms. Often on the first Sunday of the new year, we'll use a blessing from one of the psalms that offer blessing—Psalm 128, for example. We introduce it simply:

> For many of us, our whole lives are a search for blessing. We want our boss's blessing or our mother's blessing or our spouse's blessing. Sometimes we receive it. Sometimes we don't. What a gift this morning to start the new year with the blessing of God, our Heavenly Father. Would you turn toward someone nearby, look them in the eye, and repeat after me?

And then, line by line, sentence by sentence, a worship leader speaks the words of Psalm 128, and attendees repeat after her. Congregants bless each other.

Of course, this can be a bit on the edge for a first-time attendee or a strong introvert. And, as in most psalms, the images are a bit startling. As the psalm rolls along, it's poignant to see people blessing each other. It works. Maybe even *because* the psalm's images feel a bit funky in a contemporary setting, they seem to transcend an introvert's hesitation or a first-time attendee's uncertainty. Picture a father saying to his estranged adolescent son, "Blessed are all who fear the LORD" (Ps 128:1). Imagine a blue-collar union worker and a software engineer telling each other, "Blessings and prosperity will be yours" (Ps 128:2). Picture an outspoken teenager saying to her father,

"Your wife will be like a fruitful vine within your house" (Ps 128:3). Every time we get to that particular line people burst into laughter. Of course. The image is so startling they often can't even say the words. The whole room bursts into a kind of churchy pandemonium. But it's not the laughter of mocking or derision or shame. It's the laughter of delight. Dare I say, it's the laughter of blessing. And then we all seem to recover our senses together, even more committed to what we're doing. Our blessing somehow enhanced and deepened the joy. So when the psalm ends with these beautiful lines, "May you live to see your children's children" (Ps 128:6), we mean it. And we receive it in hope. Who doesn't want to give and receive such a blessing?

It's struck me more than once that in the moment of blessing, we are sending people to a world that desperately needs trained blessers. Worship informs and forms us. So when trained blessers tuck their children into bed at night, or pray a final prayer at a parent's dying bedside, or send off a son back to a difficult college situation or to a dangerous army post, we know what to say. We've learned the words in church. "The LORD bless you and keep you; the Lord make his face shine on you" (Num 6:24–25).

Several weeks ago, a relatively new attendee said with overflowing enthusiasm, "I used our blessing!" I must have looked a bit confused, so he went on, undeterred: "At a friend's anniversary celebration last night, I used the blessing we say every week at the end of church. I blessed them. And they loved it."

May you live to see your children's children,
Kevin

September (Year Two and Beyond)

On Worship as Healing

Dear Jordan,

I'm glad for your team's ongoing debate. I know it's much easier to hear about conflicting opinions than to live in the middle of them. But this one is truly a gift.

In a hundred subtle and not-so-subtle ways, our self-image (our sense of pastoral identity and calling) shapes how we lead worship services. It shapes whether we see the classic elements of the ordo as treasures or as options to pick and choose at our discretion. It shapes how we interact with our fellow worshipers. It's possible to use elements from the classic ordo or any liturgical framework in ways that suck the grace from them, or in a spirit of thinly veiled spite or hostility or boredom.

Let me offer another image for worship leaders to help your debate along. When I was a student at Fuller Seminary, there was a well-known and controversial class called "Signs, Wonders, and Church Growth." Led by John Wimber, founder of the Vineyard movement, and missiologist Peter Wagner, the class proposed that the church has always grown and loved people via extraordinary signs. These signs are mostly in the form of healing we read about in the New Testament—Peter's mother-in-law bedridden with fever, a paralytic man lowered through a ceiling by four determined friends, the blind Bartimaeus shouting from the side of the road.

As part of the class, each of us students were handed a thick three-ring binder (laptops weren't yet affordable for graduate students) overflowing with readings taken from the Bible and from church history about the healing work of God. I found it fascinating. I'd never seen biblical stories of healing systematically arranged like other church doctrines such as missiology, soteriology, and eschatology. But what really interested me, the reason I took the class, was the prospect of seeing people physically or emotionally healed.

I'll never forget the day I was sitting in a back row when one of Wimber's pastoral associates whispered in the ear of my friend and fellow student. My friend had been sitting in the chair next to me, but suddenly he was on the ground, shaking. And he kept shaking for several minutes. I sat nearby, stunned and frozen in place. This had never happened in a worship service I'd attended. The instigating whisperer knelt nearby, holding my friend's hand. When the shaking stopped, I saw tears streaming down my friend's face. And, in a great surprise to me, he gave a tender smile. His reaction to shaking was a smile!

Later that evening in his apartment, as we further discussed the experience, he confided that the pastor had whispered to him that God knew about a very specific sin in his past and had fully forgiven him. No one knew what he had done. But *he* did. And in that moment, stirred by the Holy Spirit, so did this pastor. My friend had carried his secret for years. Its toxic shame marred his relationships. It weighed down his soul and left him staggering to get through each day. And then it was, in a moment of healing grace, gone.

I thought about this again while attending a Christian Community Development Association (CCDA) conference in Detroit a while back. To say it was inspiring is to say a winter in Minnesota is cold. Young attendees were there, determined to commit their lives to a particular often-challenging neighborhood. Middle-aged folks were there, bearing the weight of having given their lives to a particular often-challenging neighborhood. And of course founder John Perkins was there too. He'd given his life to helping people of all backgrounds give their lives to serving particular often-challenging neighborhoods.

The worship leaders sang a wonderful mix of Motown soul and Christian standards all with a high-energy, culturally eclectic vibe. But what was striking to so many of us was the way their spirited mix of music and words brought healing to attendees. They intended this, of course. They knew the room overflowed with ministry leaders who had limped into the conference. They were beaten and bruised. They were weighed down by their calling, by their broken neighborhoods and hearts, and by the unexpected disappointments and the high tax of long-haul ministry. Self-consciously, deliberately, the worship leaders sought to heal the wounded attendees. Their songs brought healing. Their instruments, their voices, and their words brought healing. And it made me wonder: aren't all worship services a kind of healing?

Aren't the call to confession and words of assurance a kind of healing? We stop and reflect on the specific ways we have contributed to the mess in our world and neighborhood, and we receive grace. And we dare to imagine again that God might forgive us and call us again to be agents of shalom, to participate in our neighborhood's healing.

The simple act of passing the peace can be healing. It's not difficult to imagine a husband and wife fighting on the way to a worship service, debating if they even should remain married, let alone attend the day's worship service. So they sit through the call to worship and the opening songs in the particular brand of silence married couples perfect. Emotions simmer at a toxic temperature. The smallest slight will bring the sullen, brooding mess to boiling over. But instead, a worship leader directs them to speak to each other ancient words of life, "The peace of Christ be with you." Healing.

A sermon on an ordinary Sunday or following a riot at a local high school might be prophetic or it might be pastoral. Or it might be prophetic *and* pastoral *and* healing, like so many given by Dr. Martin Luther King Jr. Isn't it healing to imagine and step bravely toward a country characterized by harmony instead of racism? Healing.

And a benediction can be healing. We live so much of our life hoping and aching and striving for a blessing. And then at the end of the worship service, there it is. We can cease our striving and simply receive it. Healing.

I have a good friend who lost her spouse a couple years ago. It's all she can do to show up to any public place even now. Friends expect she's moved to a new place, that she's getting on with her life. But each day she lives with a gaping hole in her heart. She tells me, "It's like I don't have any skin. My whole life feels raw and vulnerable." But one of the few places she doesn't feel this exquisite pain is a worship service. Healing.

Worship at that Detroit conference was healing. It made many of us wonder if that can be true of all Christian worship. People in every setting, formal or informal, suburban or urban, big city or small town, attend worship knowingly or unknowingly, longing for healing.

All this takes us back to that ancient image of the pastoral vocation, one you and your team and every worship leader can claim: to be a doctor of souls. Sometimes that means we do surgery, removing cancerous and harmful growths. Sometimes that means we need to speak warning truth, when what seems a harmless peccadillo is really a toxic and long-standing pattern. Sometimes we speak encouragement, lifting the sorrowful to hope or inviting the broken to new life. Always, during every worship service, in music and words and Eucharistic invitation, we offer healing.

When we speak the beautiful words of the timeless liturgy or when we say a simple frame before or after these words, we can do so as an agent of healing.

Yours,
Kevin

On Liturgical Time and the Hiddenness of Formation

Dear Jordan,

I'm convinced the worship frames we're designing and using are of great benefit. I'm convinced the elements of the classic, time-tested worship ordo are inherently and robustly missional. I'm convinced these frames will have practical traction in people's lives, including our own.

But this seems like a good time to pause for what business leaders sometimes call "expectation management." Spiritual formation is slow. Sometimes people have a Damascus road experience—lightning strikes, and their world suddenly changes. But many times, dare I say *most* of the time, it happens slowly. Maybe that's why many congregations tossed aside the classic elements. Not *seeing* visible and dramatic effects in the lives of most worshipers, they assume nothing is happening.

Spiritual change is often slow. And hidden. But it happens. This past week a thoughtful new attendee at our church came forward for communion. In response to receiving the bread and wine, we suggest participants say, "Thanks be to God." But this incredibly thoughtful person was smiling from ear to ear as she said to me, "This is my first communion!" The miracle of grace always astonishes and delights!

But it's also messy. We are careful to explain (frame) worship elements. But even then people don't follow instructions. Did I tell you about the person who received the bread during communion and immediately popped it into her mouth? When she saw the cup and realized we celebrate by intinction, she popped the bread *out* of her mouth and started to dip it in the chalice. The first time this happened we were too shocked to move. Now experience has made us watchful and wary. We are ready to help them find a better way.

In faith—the kind that is sure of what we cannot see,
Kevin

On Being Natural and Personable—or Faking It

Dear Jordan,

As you know, our video call ended with a spirited discussion on the best practices of worship leaders (or framers). The next morning a wonderful email entered my inbox. I hesitated at first to forward it because it might sound self-aggrandizing. You know firsthand that after getting an email like this you want to run laps around the church parking lot in delight! And you know that in any context this email is balanced by other conversations that leave you wanting to sneak out the back door. In other words, there's plenty each day to lift our spirits and to keep us humble. Having said that, I pass it on because of the great delight it is to share between trusted friends, but also because it gives a kind of vision and practical direction for the how to section of our conversation.

Dear Kevin,

A blessing to you!

I've often thought to write, and am prompted to now after just reading your latest blog on the *Reformed Worship* website. I loved it. As I did the one on weekly communion. And I still have good memories of my visit to your congregation on the Sunday after Christmas last year, when I was out to see my friends. I loved then how you led the liturgy, and am grateful for how you are mentoring young seminarians in their preaching and worship leadership roles.

When I went home, I went on the website and was disappointed that the liturgy itself was not available online, just the sermon. I would have loved to hear how you invited and then led the congregation in reciting all of Psalm 136 along with you as happened that Sunday, making it joyful. So naturally. And how you led from the Word to the table, inviting everyone in such a way that everyone from a first-timer to someone like me, who's been coming to the table for years, felt so hospitably welcomed to the table. It's that kind of thing I would love to see and hear on the website too.

Have you given any thought to extending your web page to include more of that kind of worship leadership in addition to the sermon? I know there would be copyright issues on the music, but I'm thinking more of the teaching possibilities of the other spoken parts of worship. We often talk where I work about the importance of "in-between words" that introduce, invite, help transition from one action to another. You made it sound effortless, but I know that great preparation and skill are involved. Only when practiced can that skill appear effortless. But this is what so many need to have modeled, just as preaching is modeled.

Well, next time you're in town, I'd love to have coffee or a further conversation on all this, if these thoughts move you in any way towards thinking how something like this could happen.

Thanks for listening!

God bless you now and always, Kevin.

Emily

P.S. I'm so sure, Jordan, that you'd love Emily. She embodies everything we've been talking about and will want to accent on our retreat. She's thoughtful and wise, ready to learn from people younger or older than her, from any tradition or ethnic group. I'm happy if this email is just between us, but if you think the entire group can benefit, you are welcome to send it on.

On Nurturing a Community of Missional Worship Leaders

Dear Jordan,

What a joy to be together last week with your team! Erin's pizza. Santiago's guitar. Eliene, Jiao-Long, and Milagra's beautiful vocals. Your waffles at breakfast. And who could ever forget Zendaya leading us in Welly dances! Such joy! And now we have proof that, like me, you have two left feet!

You asked me to send along the notes from our final session—the flip chart exercise where we listed best practices moving forward. Here they are. The point of all this is to further develop as a team, to deepen your trust and joy and sense of mission.

I understand that you passed on Emily's email to everyone. I hope in reading her words you see how similar her list is to yours as a group—no small thing to realize when you consider her vast insight and the multi-layered experience she has leading worship. Here's the list from our time together:

> *What to avoid:*
> Reading frames in a formal way
> Explaining rather than framing
> In-house language
> One kind of worship leader
> Ad-libbing
> Parochialism
> Long frames regularly
> Stiff discomfort
> Rigid correctness
> Perfectionistic tendencies
>
> *What to celebrate:*
> Memorized or internalized frames
> Winsome, short frames
> Contagious hospitality
> Leadership from all generations
> Teamwork in creating global and multicultural experiences
> A winning sentence or two

Natural demeanor that welcomes
Joy
Trusting grace
Some best (or possible) practices:
Preparation that includes advance drafts and feedback
Evaluations that celebrate grace, and maybe video review
Inviting church leaders, elders, and deacons to participate
Memorizing the frames
Giving people permission to be prepared and imperfect
Inviting manner, looking people in the eye, memorization
Authenticity

One way to summarize this is "embodied grace." During worship, you're speaking about what you genuinely live. My only encouragement is to continue to meet together as a team and to speak with candor and grace. I know you're just getting started, but what you have is wonderful!

With fondness,
Kevin

P.S. I did hear some talk about another day together—to take our white board list and design a retreat around these practices. If you make your waffles, I'm all in!

On the Unexpected and When Ministry Doesn't Go Well

Dear Jordan,

This past Sunday at our congregation's morning worship service, an elementary school brother and sister were scheduled to say the call to worship together. They've done it before, reciting part of a psalm together, shifting the microphone between the two of them, and it is a sheer delight to behold. As one long-term attendee told me once, "I'd come to church just to hear them recite a psalm." It's so effortless, so joyful—delivered with their entire being.

On this particular Sunday, their mom and dad couldn't guide them to the front of the church and up to the microphone. So these two small saints sat beside me. At the appointed time (we place a subtle but visible cue on a PowerPoint slide to guide all participants), the young brother left his seat ahead of his sister and started toward the front. But en route he noticed something outside the large windows that frame our sanctuary. A bird? A flower? A plane? The casino across the field (yes, our church has a view of a casino!)?

Like any self-respecting eight-year-old, he stopped to look. But his sister, not seeing what he saw and so focused on going on to the platform, nudged him in the ribs. It was a gentle sibling nudge, well-placed and well-intended. She only wanted to get him started in the direction of the microphone, where they would recite Psalm 149 together as a call to worship.

Her brother, momentarily forgetting where he was, responded as any brother might to an unexpected sisterly nudge in the ribs: with a hard shove aimed to escalate the disagreement. He looked at her with the kind of facial expression siblings perfect—a mix of disdain, disregard, superiority, ire, and physical resistance.

But then he seemed to catch himself, to instantly remember where he was—near the front of church with hundreds of eyes observing him. His face flushed. Now realizing the nudge didn't warrant a full expression of sibling rivalry, he sensed his sister might actually have been helpful. So they moved forward, bounced up the stairs to the platform, recited the psalm antiphonally, and ended jointly with a cheerful, "Praise the Lord," just as they had rehearsed it.

Observing all this with me, a wise witness of life and someone who dearly loves these two whispered to me, "That's a parable for the Christian life."

Indeed.

They're good. Very good. But even good people aren't perfect. And sometimes worship doesn't go as we plan or expect.

Imperfectly yours,
Kevin

On Living with Mistakes, and Laughter

Dear Jordan,

I thought that story of sibling rivalry might resonate with you. It happens, doesn't it? Despite our best planning, some things just happen in the actual moment.

A few years ago, one of our pastors was reciting a psalm during the service. Suddenly, right in the middle of reciting, it was gone, suddenly evaporated from his memory. It is, of course, one of the disadvantages of memorizing (or, as one of our elders puts it, "soaring without a net"). Most of the time, if one can wait patiently and calmly, the text reappears on the screen of our mind, and we can continue. But once in a while it does not. As in this case. So the pastor simply said, "In the name of the Father, the Son, and the Holy Spirit." Only a few of us knew that wasn't the original intent.

At a Christmas Eve worship service last year, one of our pastors was reciting the familiar story of Luke 2 to the children and to everyone else in attendance. Our service follows the traditional lessons and carols framework that started in Cambridge, England, in the early 1900s. We find that saying the text from memory adds a subtle but marked power to the biblical storytelling.

The pastor-reciter made it through Quirinius and the innkeeper and the swaddling clothes. But his mind went blank after he said, "The shepherds said to one another . . ." So he simply smiled, paused, and said, "There's more!" Everyone laughed—not with the laughter of mocking accusation, but with the laughter that says we honor someone who speaks from memory. In his case he remembered the "more" and got the shepherds to Mary and Joseph.

Laughter and gospel joy.

It was the famous London preacher Charles Spurgeon who, when criticized for saying something funny while preaching, said it was "less a crime to cause a momentary laughter than a half-hour's profound slumber."[1]

A few months ago, I was presiding over the Eucharist celebration. We had made a subtle change in the way we presented the elements at our table; the changes were designed to help us be more hospitable to people who need gluten-free bread.

I knew about these changes, and they seemed incremental. But after repeating those precious words hundreds of times, suddenly while reciting the Institution from 1 Corinthians I got it all backwards. I began not with the bread as Jesus and Paul and thousands of years of Christian tradition began, but with the cup. Of course, there's no going back at that point. We have Eucharist weekly. I've recited Paul's invitation hundreds of times. But suddenly it was gone!

After the service, I was relating this inner tangle to our associate pastor. He's a keen observer and had noticed my gaffe. As we chuckled together, he said, "There's more. During the invitation to receive the bread you said it was poured out for us." Oops. I'm quite sure bread is never poured. There's no frame in the world that can rescue that mistake.

During the first week of Advent, one of our stellar worship leaders stepped forward on the front platform of the sanctuary, and the garland that had been so carefully arranged at the front fell down in a ripple, like dominoes falling one after another. It must have taken a full sixty seconds, slowly

---

1. Spurgeon, *Autobiography*, 2:155.

cascading down piece by piece, each pausing just for a moment before falling in line. The worship leader handled it gracefully. He simply watched it fall, smiled, and spoke his worship frame just as he had planned it. And then he walked off the platform. It turns out you don't need garland in the right place to continue a worship service.

Did I ever tell you about the Sunday evening service years ago when I was a pastor in Minnesota? Each week a child would take home a "mystery box" from the morning service and return to the evening service with something inside. As part of the service, I would open the mystery box and give an impromptu children's message on the contents. The congregants loved it. So did the kids.

That Sunday the family bringing the mystery item was especially anxious. On previous Sundays children had placed much-loved dolls, toy soldiers, and a lucky rabbit's foot in the box. Often I'd give the box a gentle shake to try to get a clue to the possible contents. But that particular Sunday, when I gave a gentle shake, the family who brought the item started to levitate in alarm. A family pet was in the box! I shook Sugar, their dearly beloved hamster.

Yes, unexpected things happen in worship services. And yes, it might be fun at the retreat to tell such tales. We want to plan and prepare, to be thoughtful and wise. But we don't want to pretend we always get it right. And knowing such tales and foibles can give us grace to go on.

Spurgeon was right. Laughter is good for a congregation. Maybe it's a sign of a healthy community. Wasn't it G. K. Chesterton who said, "Angels can fly because they can take themselves lightly"?[2]

There's no reason to be unprepared. But neither is there any reason to be anxious or tense. It is all about grace, after all.

Grateful to be on the journey of learning and worshiping together,
Kevin

P.S. Sometimes as worship leaders we can take solace in that everyone in every vocation makes mistakes. Kindergarten teachers don't always remember their students' names. All-star baseball players hit with a 70 percent failure rate. Great Broadway actors forget key lines. During the last season of *Game of Thrones*, a Starbucks coffee cup was spotted on the set—but not until the episode aired. Showrunner David Benioff said, "At first I couldn't believe it, and then it was an embarrassment because, 'How we did not see this in the middle of the shot?' And then it was just funny. This one is just a mistake, and it's kind of funny to us now."[3]

2. Chesterton, *Orthodoxy*, ch. 7.
3. Bruney, "The *Game of Thrones* Showrunners."

On Christ the King Sunday

Dear Jordan,

At last. We've reached the final Sunday of the liturgical year. I'm glad you found this a bit easier subject than unwrapping the mystery of our triune God on Trinity Sunday. You captured the heart of this week with your frame. Nicely done. You asked for a frame we use as an additional example for our upcoming retreat. Here you go:

> Some people say the church should not be political. Others say the church *should* be political. What do you think?
>
> Throughout the Bible, the main image of God is that of king. In Old Testament stories, psalms and prophets, God is king. And when New Testament writers said "Jesus is Lord," they challenged an empire where everyone knew Caesar was Lord.
>
> To put it another way, to follow Christ as King is to be political. He is first. That doesn't mean the church should be *partisan*. We may disagree about the best strategies to bring about world peace. But behind our strategies is full political agreement: Christ is King!

I know, that frame might generate some charged conversation in any congregation. And it might be wiser to use in some settings rather than others. But it only fills me with more anticipation about our retreat conversation.

I'm delighted to be seeing you this weekend. My anticipation abounds! And what a great joy it is that we aren't really in charge, but simply point repeatedly and gracefully to the One who is.

Kevin

On a Workbook for Framing Worship

Dear Jordan,

What a great idea! Your team is so inventive.

Let me make sure I'm understanding. Your group would like to write a workbook for other worship teams so we can share what we're learning together and glean wisdom from other congregations in a wide variety of settings? Various members of your group will plan individual sections, some working on the liturgical year, others working through the most typical classic worship elements? And you're asking for input from me on each section as we go along?

The book is to have two parts, right? A section on framing various elements and then a second section on framing best practices? Of course, I'm delighted!

Let's move forward with your team's suggestion that we give the workbook an encouraging, informal feel to heighten the creativity of your emerging group of leaders.

And yes again to your idea to invite neighboring congregations from a variety of traditions to give input. Such a multilayered and multicultural learning environment will benefit us all. Each tradition will bring their own accents and expertise to our learning. What fun we'll have as we work together!

I look forward to the ongoing conversation!

Gratefully,
Kevin

Final Letter To the Reader: On Being Jordan

Dear Friend,

Who is Jordan? Jordan is my good friend. A person with a deep passion for God and a deep desire to see people's lives transformed by the Holy Spirit. Jordan is male and female, conservative and liberal. Jordan is the name of one of my seminary students and of my cousin's son. Jordan is of Mexican, Native American, African, and European descent, with the sensibilities of an artist and the instincts of an engineer. In previous employment, Jordan was a barista and a wine connoisseur, a stay-at-home parent and a retiree. Jordan is young and old—timeless, really. Jordan is you. Jordan is me. Jordan is someone specific and a compilation of many of my friends. Jordan is beloved, called, and equipped for this amazing vocation of leading worship in a way that points to the ongoing treasures of grace. I can't wait for you two to meet.

Thanks for who you are. And thanks for answering the call to lead worship faithfully with your humble curiosity and teachable spirit.

God bless you, Jordan!
Kevin

PART TWO

WISDOM

It is in the process of being worshipped that God communicates His presence.

—C. S. LEWIS, *REFLECTIONS ON THE PSALMS*

Give thanks to the LORD, for he is good.
His love endures forever.

—PSALM 136:1

What We Carry into (Framing) Worship

WHEN TIM O'BRIEN RETURNED from military service in the Vietnam War, he was disheartened at how little people back home knew about the reality of the war and its toll on people. But rather than starting a fiery partisan debate or combative conversation he wrote a story, *The Things They Carried*.

Based on his experiences in the 23rd Infantry Division, the characters in his semi-fictional autobiography become the men of the Alpha Company. Each man carries what they need to survive physically and emotionally, what makes them who they are. Over time, as O'Brien weaves his story, we come to understand them by knowing what they carry.

Platoon leader Lt. Jimmy Cross carries his unbridled love for Martha, the girl he dated immediately before shipping off from the States. Lonely and adrift, walking through tropical rainstorms and suffocating heat, he carries her letters. He is smitten with her, but she doesn't return his affection. Company medic Bob "Rat" Kiley carries malaria tablets, morphine, and his own personal taste for cruelty. Norman Bowker carries memories of the night he was unable to save his fellow soldier from dying. The memories haunt him and make him unable to move on. Henry Dobbins carries his superstition. So he wears "his girlfriend's panty hose wrapped around his neck as a comforter."[1] Jimmy's best friend, Kiowa, a devout Baptist, carries his Bible and "his grandmother's distrust of white people."[2] Ted Lavender carries a supply of first-rate dope and the tranquilizers he needs to survive emotionally. "They all carried ghosts," O'Brien writes.[3]

What do you carry into worship, and why? A friend of mine told me about a chapel service he recently attended at an evangelical college. The speaker of the day wore the distinctive clothes of his cutting-edge congregation. Defying the ninety-degree temperature outside and the blazing lights

---

1. O'Brien, *The Things They Carried*, 9.
2. O'Brien, *The Things They Carried*, 3.
3. O'Brien, *The Things They Carried*, 9.

on stage, he wore the checked flannel in vogue among the hip worshipers of his neighborhood. Knowingly or not, he carried expectations about acceptance and the apparel required to receive it.

Another friend was getting ready to preach for the first time. To prepare, she had listened to a lifetime of sermons. She had spoken repeatedly as an academic. She had read commentaries to understand the text, consulted with her pastor to understand the context, and attended several preaching labs to hone her delivery. It was then that she found herself considering what to wear. Throughout her life she had heard mixed messages about whether women should preach in worship settings. Wearing a dress was more than a fashion choice; it was a symbol of her status as a woman and of God's acceptance of that reality.

Early in our congregation's life, I often carried my guitar into worship. This was unfortunate for those who came. Some things are better left home. But without that guitar, we'd have sung *a cappella*—and my singing skills are several steps lower than my guitar-playing ability. A fellow musician from those early days carried his instrument too, as well as the deep, half-spoken desire for our worship to mirror the profoundly charismatic healing ministry of the church in which he came to faith as an adult. He had deep wounds he carried everywhere from episodes in his adolescence. More than anything, he carried cravings that worship would heal him.

Another companion from those early days carried his vintage electric-red Fender guitar into worship. He began touring the country in his late teens, playing music in all sorts of venues. A consummate rock and roll musician, Gene learned to work the night club crowd, get people to buy drinks, and be invited back. His bands opened for Steppenwolf, Creedence Clearwater Revival, and other music legends. He's a sweet-spirited person people instantly like. One attendee in our congregation remarked wistfully that when Gene plays his electric guitar in church, "We should charge a two-drink minimum." Gene brings to worship his own brand of musical expertise, and by his frank admission, an initial bewilderment about church music.

Everyone, it seems, brings musical expectations to church. Two months ago I welcomed two first-time attendees sitting in the back row of our sanctuary. I greeted them as warmly as I knew how, saying I hoped they'd feel welcome, and should they ever have any questions about church or faith, we'd do our best to answer them. One responded in a tight growl, "Is what we see on the front platform an indication of what we will experience in the worship service?" Somewhat puzzled, I turned to look at the platform. I saw people, musicians, and worship leaders in final preparations. I saw the classic pulpit and sacramental furniture, recently constructed from reclaimed wood more than a hundred years old. Then I followed his eyes to the source of his growl, a Pearl drum kit. In case I missed his sharp point, he continued, "Will there be loud drums in this service?" I responded, perhaps more curtly than intended, "We often feature percussion in our service, and I assume we will today. The volume matches the musical intentions of the day." He remained, unsmiling, for the entire service. He has not returned—yet. One attendee expects classic hymnody, another hip hop, or country, or Bill Gaither, or Taizé, or Hillsong, or gospel, or classical music. People carry expectations for a pipe organ, a jazz organ, or a mouth organ.

One recent attendee is still emotionally recovering from a megachurch she describes as "more business than church." Another hopes there's enough accountability to fend off the financial and relational chaos her previous congregation slogged through. A few years ago I attended an English service in Beijing. The music, seen through the overly analytical view I often carry, was a clippity-cloppety, Americanized version of vintage hymns and dated "contemporary" music. The sermon was a download of dense information, more college lecture than good news. Worship leaders asked first-time guests to stand; they sang us a welcome song from the 1980s I found slightly awkward. If this congregation were in our neighborhood, my guess is fewer than fifteen people would attend each week. But in Beijing, that six-month-old worship service overflowed with hundreds of enthusiastic and youthful worshipers. It was a delight and a wonder. Obviously what people carry to worship in mainline China is profoundly different from what some of us carry in Sacramento.

A much-loved seminary professor of pastoral care once told me, "People are angrier than they have ever been before. They take their anger to church, lay it at the feet of the pastor, and say, 'It's your fault.'" Years ago a music leader confessed to me her abiding envy of her sister. Her own life was a struggle, but her sister seemed carefree. Her own relationships were complicated and full of drama; her sister's seemed amiable and life-giving. She struggled off and on with depression; her sister seemed easygoing and affable. And maybe worst of all, she trained vigorously to squeeze all the talent she could from her vocal genetics while her sister had the voice of an angel. A colleague told me about a mutual friend, a skilled and thoughtful pastor, who was emotionally beaten over a six-month period of ministry through no fault of his own. Now he brings his wounds and his sadness to church. We carry emotions to worship: anger, envy, sadness.

Author Anne Lamott writes that she and her family carried with them their father's cold Presbyterian upbringing. Henri Nouwen, a Dutch Catholic priest and prolific author on spirituality, carried hidden the secret that he was gay, as well as the voices of friends urging him to come out. A pastor I know carries with him his adoption as a child and a lifetime of separation anxiety. One of my seminary students carries his past as a Mexican gangster, prisoner, and self-proclaimed violent punk. An immigrant carries bewilderment at new customs and cultures. Jesus carried with him his refugee childhood, his peasant upbringing, and the voice of his heavenly Father: "You are my son, whom I love; with you I am well pleased."[4]

We too carry voices sometimes: the voice of our own expectations and failures, or the voice of our hidden, compelling desires. Maybe we carry the voice of a mentor warning us about worship hazards, cautioning against patterns too formal or too Catholic, or against reading a book like this. Maybe you carry voices that warn against watering down the gospel, or the tradition, or mingling with people who vote or understand worship differently than you. Most of the time, as we begin to develop our own particular worship voice (and that of our congregation), we try on other voices, familiar or unfamiliar: a worship leader we admire, a preacher we find fascinating, a leader whose congregation has experienced pronounced growth.

Growing up, I heard two voices about praying the psalms. The voice of my blue-collar father saying, "The psalms we sing in church sound like funeral music," and the voice of my immigrant maternal grandmother quietly reveling in them as sustenance for her widowed soul. It's no surprise, having heard those conflicting voices, that it took me more than fifteen years of ministry to sort out how the psalms might work in our emerging congregation.

Do you think the first disciples carried inner voices as well? Did the Apostle Peter worship with a voice of both failure and forgiveness? Did the Apostle Paul carry both regret and conviction? Did Jesus' mother Mary carry both grief and hope?

Knowing what longtime and first-time congregants carry with them helps you understand them, lead them, and create worship frames for them, for their deepest selves. Just as the narrator of *The Things They Carried* enables us to understand Jimmy and the rest of Alpha Company, as worship leaders we're invited to know attendees' beliefs, motives, and idols as well as (or better than) they do themselves.

Like the soldiers in Jimmy's platoon, we worship leaders carry our own stories with us, even as we plan worship. Maybe *especially* as we plan worship. I am the grandson of immigrants and the son of a janitor. I grew up in the church attended by my grandparents and great-grandparents. I have been a pastor of the same congregation for almost three decades. I attended three seminaries. My neighborhood overflows with secular people. Those

4. Mark 1:11, NIV.

realities form my story. They are part of what I bring to worship and to lead-ing and framing worship. In a similar way, where you live or were raised, whether in Durham, North Carolina, or Vigo, Spain, or Red Deer, Alberta, affects what you carry—maybe for generations. A Spaniard whose ances-tors fought Napoleon and the Moors, a granddaughter of slaves bought and abused by pious Christian owners, and a Native American whose relatives were introduced to a contaminated mix of the gospel and white suprema-cy—all inherit stories. We carry our own stories and those of generations before us to worship.

Once I asked one of our church's college interns about a certain wise worship leader he had as a professor. In the asking, I was celebrating this leader's profoundly life-giving effect on our congregation and literally thou-sands of others. The intern replied glibly and off-handedly, "I had him a couple times as a professor, and I've learned everything I need to from him." The intern carries a pronounced (over) confidence into worship, and maybe a marked lack of curiosity.

Having listened to many leaders and to my own heart, I find we also often carry our *againstness* into worship. We are against people who vote differently than us, against people of a different branch of Christianity, against people who went to seminary or those who did not, against people we immediately like or dislike, against people who don't share our taste in music or liturgy or attire suitable for worship leading. We might be against prepared prayers or impromptu music, against changes to the liturgy or against worship leaders of a certain age. At a church leadership conference I attended, several speakers spoke assuredly that the surest and fastest way to grow a church in the United States was to have an up-front worship leader-ship team with no one over thirty. I'm against their againstness. But I also realize, with some soul-searching, that I'm against other things: stuffy ritual, formal ceremony, empty posturing, and in-house worship that assumes all attendees are lifelong Christians.

Some things we grow weary of carrying are anxiety, performance pres-sure, a desire for widespread approval, spiritual dysfunction, racism, narrow parochialism, and the scorning voice of rejection or dismissal. I have several friends who were forced out of the churches they served. One was asked to leave the church he began after twenty-five years of fruitful ministry. Another led a church through two decades of phenomenal growth, from several dozen people to over 2,000. He did all this through long work weeks, personal and family sacrifice, and the grace of God, only to have the church board replace him with a younger version of himself while he was going through a season of emotional winter. Rejection is a heavy load to carry. And it doesn't always get lighter over time.

There are also things we *want* to carry, especially as we frame worship. Consider a short list of worship convictions I want to carry into worship that can help us all become adept framers:[5]

Worship is for mission
Worship is ancient
Worship is historic
Worship is slow
Worship is an encounter; it is about presence
Worship is new
Worship is orderly
Worship is messy
Worship is relational
Worship happens together
Worship is global
Worship is spiritually formative
Worship is timeless
Worship is beautiful
Worship is overwhelmingly mysterious
Worship is experiential
Worship makes room for doubts
Worship is work
Worship is catholic
Worship is wet
Worship is strange and can feel cultish
Worship is verbal
Worship is communal
Worship is personal
Worship is healing
Worship is to be a healing encounter with the living God
Worship is pastoral

I want to carry these convictions into worship. It is not a complete list. But it's a start.

A friend once asked a gifted veteran pastor what he thought about on Sunday mornings while waiting for the church service to begin. Without needing time to consider, as if this thought had occurred to him many times, he answered, "Why does anyone come?" He went on to reflect, "No one can make a person come to a worship service; it's always a marvel when they do." He carries gratitude into worship, with a sense of profound dependence on the Holy Spirit. I'd like to carry that too.

---

5. Thanks to Tim Blackmon for alerting me to this list, inferred from the Letters section.

Some weeks on my ten-minute journey to church I feel anxiety rising inside. Occasionally this is conscious; I can sense its brooding gloom. Other weeks it's unconscious. I'm ruminating distractedly, silently rehearsing my sermon, or thinking of a certain announcement or upcoming conversation. I want to be prepared. I want to do the best I can. But sometimes that worthy aspiration transforms into performance (or other kinds of) anxiety. I no longer want to be good for the sake of the kingdom of God, but just for the sake of being good. Or just for the sake of me. When I'm aware of this anxiety, I try to remind myself, "I want to love these folks. Lord, let me love them." I want to carry love into worship.

I'd also like to carry a buoyant expectancy. Over the years I'm amazed by the ordinary and extraordinary moments of palpable grace that happen before or in or after a worship service. Recently a senior citizen in our church found me before the Sunday service began. He jumped right in: "At this time tomorrow I'll be under," referring to his upcoming cancer surgery. I promised we as a community were praying for him and for his wife, who has her own health issues. I knew they were feeling vulnerable about this next season of life. He relayed some of the next morning's details, the arrival time, the robotic surgery, and the specific friends who would be in the waiting room. With conviction he said, "You know that blessing you say at the end of every worship service? My wife and I said that blessing over each other last night. It meant a lot to us both." And then he said words I may never forget: "When you say that blessing today, could you look at me? I need to remember God is with me." And there it was, an unexpected moment of beauty and grace.

There are so many good things to carry. My list goes on and on: I'd like to carry an unending delight in the gospel, self-deprecating humor, a lack of self-importance, an empathetic acceptance of people unlike me, and a palpable sense of my baptismal identity.

What about you? And what about your congregation?

Worship is a way of seeing the world in the light of God.

—ABRAHAM JOSHUA HESCHEL

Shout for joy to the LORD, all the earth.
Worship the Lord with gladness.

—PSALM 100

Seven Proverbs for Leading
and Framing Worship

THE EMMY AWARD-WINNING TELEVISION show *The West Wing* was in crisis mode. Real-life terrorists had wreaked horror on New York's World Trade Center and on the United States' psyche. Radicals crashed a plane into the Pentagon and targeted the White House. Fear reigned. The thin trust between people of varying backgrounds evaporated. People were visibly and vocally anxious and uncertain. How could a mere television show address a global reality? But then, how could a television show about an imaginary but palpably realistic cadre of characters working in the White House *not* address this real-life calamity? Could this quick-witted, fast-paced, cleverly worded show spin quickly to address a real-life trauma? Could it do in two weeks what is typically done over months? Could it be true to its overarching narrative while also being true to what was happening in its national neighborhood right then and there? It could. And it did.

In response to a national tragedy, *The West Wing* writers invented an entirely new episode, aptly titled "Isaac and Ishmael." In two weeks, they wrote, rehearsed, and filmed—an insane task for network television. They designed a plot faithful not only to the main story arc of both their show's past season and their carefully crafted upcoming season, but also to the internal chaos viewers were feeling.

The plot: The West Wing of the White House goes on lockdown when security discovers a suspected terrorist working there. A group of high school students visiting the White House that day get herded to an underground cafeteria. Stuck together with the president's staff, some peanut butter, and a few apple slices, they wait in vulnerability for the all-clear. As they wait, they begin to debate the issue on everyone's mind: terrorism. The students ask leading questions, showing their anger at Muslims but also exposing the double standards of members of the White House staff. Eventually even the president and first lady join the exchange.

Before the episode aired, cast members introduced (we might say *framed*) the episode. Speaking out of character, as their real selves, together they simply and artfully explained how the episode would speak both to the current reality and the show's broader story line. This episode would both break continuity *and* be part of the whole. (Regular programming would return to its third season the following week.)

Martin Sheen, known to *The West Wing* viewers as President Jed Bartlett, began. Rob Lowe, Allison Janney, and Bradley Whitford took turns naming (framing) what viewers were about to witness, an episode both part of the whole and all its own.[1]

As you might expect with any art form, some critics hated the episode, believing it abandoned the series' gripping story line and the believability of its characters. They panned the premise and complained that the episode had become a play in which actors deliver well-rehearsed, caricatured lines, turning them into unsubtle lectures. But others found it spellbinding, a testament to what skilled people can do on short notice to respond thoughtfully and helpfully to the reality around them. Some marveled, "Isn't this exactly what television is *supposed* to do?"

Both the episode and its framing parallel how worship leaders are called to speak to and live out the ongoing, timeless story of worship at our specific moment in time. The church's liturgy has had 2,000 years of practice in doing exactly that.

In this book, I call worship leaders to work at the ever-new intersection of God's overarching story line and the ever-changing realities of a specific neighborhood and congregation. To be faithful to both the overarching story line and comprehensible to secular people with no Christian memory. To combine the overarching story line with the ancient practices that spiritually form individuals and congregations over time. To be like *The West Wing*'s savvy television practitioners, who were faithful to both the overall series and the specific moment in time so a viewer could watch and understand without any previous context or knowledge.

Wise worship leaders love their congregations and their Lord by embodying, living, and naming (framing) specific proverbs that guide them in winsomely inviting both spiritual novices and veterans to take in the timeless gospel good news. Let's review several foundational proverbs that worship leaders might prioritize as they live their calling.[2]

1. Introduction to "Isaac and Ishmael."

2. If you've already read the "Letters" part of this book, you might imagine this as a list that Benjamin, the expert verger at Westminster Abbey, might prioritize as he trains new vergers—bearings that he outlines and models, teaching that an astute verger learns to hold in tension all of them at once.

Worship spiritually forms all worshipers.

Last week our youth pastor, who understands deeply our congregation's worship and ecclesiastical DNA, asked a profound and important question at our staff meeting. We were seated together in our atrium (the first space people enter as they walk into our building) with Henri Nouwen's *The Return of the Prodigal Son* open in our laps. Guided by Nouwen's words, we reflected on the replica of Rembrandt's painting of the same name, inspired by Luke 15, that hangs in our church's welcoming space. Sharing our own thoughts about the beauty before us, we reveled in Nouwen's own journey, seeing himself first as the prodigal younger son and then as the angry and anxious elder son before finally accepting the challenge of spiritual adulthood. Earlier in that same meeting, we were talking about the logistics of baptizing eight adolescents and guiding five professions of faith/confirmations during worship. Seeing the fragility and uncertainty of adolescents' faith even as they were taking the next steps of Jesus-following, he asked a vital question: "Does it ever really happen?" When we answered with quizzical expressions, he rephrased the question: "Does anyone ever become the father in this painting as Nouwen outlined? Do people actually become spiritually mature adults, or are we stuck, forever vacillating between the childish behavior of spiritual runaways and that of religious overachievers incipiently pushing God away?"

Understanding his question more fully, we were struck by the answer that came to all of us at once: Of course it does. Not always. But sometimes. And surely. How do we know? Because, we told him, we see it happening in you. Then we outlined the specific spiritual growth we were seeing in his character and speech and bearing. We followed with stories of other attendees through the years, examples of people who had undoubtedly been transformed by gospel grace.

Having healthy relationships, attending seminary, teaching the Bible, leading a youth ministry, and participating in worship *formed* him. Over the seven years he has spent in our congregation, he's become a deeper, wiser, gospel version of his true self. On seeing him lead worship a couple of years ago, a service where he spoke a psalm from memory, one of his college professors was struck with a surprised "What happened to him?!"

That staff meeting our conversation continued, and we expressed again our deep hope and belief that worship will continue to spiritually form the group of adolescents about to be baptized. In fact, it reminded us of one of chief reasons we no longer baptize folks in backyard Jacuzzis. In the early years of our congregation we would say tongue in cheek that we were a Jacuzzi church. Rather than baptizing with formal baptismal fonts—don't they seem more appropriate for hand washing?—or at locations staked out in rivers—often cold and a bit treacherous—we loved the warm, hot-tub immersion into the life of Jesus following. But believing baptism to be a means of grace, both in the receiving and in the witnessing, we longed for our entire congregation to witness every baptism. So we moved the sacrament back to the worship space. For the same reason, we no longer have high school students go to their own teaching time during the worship service, and it's why children still dismissed to age-appropriate teaching now return to join the entire congregation for weekly Eucharist. We believe it's formative for them to participate fully in worship, even when—maybe especially when—they worship with people *unlike* them.

One of my friends, a devoted pastor who faithfully nurtured his congregation from the ground up only to have it swallowed almost completely by a fast-growing megachurch in his neighborhood, has a favorite phrase he likes to repeat about formation and worship: "What we win them *by* is what we win them *to*."

Another church plant in our city recruited a series of famous speakers to launch the congregation. Every month or so they would do an advertising and recruiting blitz. Everyone in the city knew what they were doing and who would be there. The congregation lasted three years, until they could no longer afford such speakers. What we win them *by* is what we win them *to*.

Times I witness and remember that worship forms all worshipers:

- When a youth leader asks wise questions about adolescent formation and worship

- When a child participating in Eucharist hears and receives, "The body of Christ for you" and "The blood of Christ for you"

- When a congregation alters their baptism practice with a view to deeper spiritual formation

- When a wise pastor leads her entire congregation in an act of remembering baptism

- When earworms planted by church musicians spontaneously come to mind on a Wednesday morning

- When a worship planning team expands conversation about worship to include new voices: people of different countries and ages and languages and economic backgrounds

In worship we receive grace.

I hear (and overhear) a lot of conversations about different types of new and rebirthed congregations. As someone who began a new congregation, I am always sympathetic—and curious. In the days our congregation began, missiologists and pastoral practitioners were talking a lot about meeting "felt needs." More recently some leaders have expounded the difference between "attractional worship" and "incarnational worship." Others contrast attractional churches, missional communities, and microchurches. As a long-time pastor, I'm fascinated by the dazzling variety of the church across the globe and throughout history. And I'm sympathetic to anyone who feels the need to push against a long-practiced or assumed model for worship and ministry. Such pushing often helps people articulate the contrast between what they have so far experienced in a congregation or in their lifetime with what they hope to experience in this new or renewed congregation. A new model or fresh terminology or a favorite author or leader might help them envision and live the specific framework they intend for ministering in their neighborhood. When I hear or read about a new model or renewed model, I often find the same question rising inside: how do worshipers in this new gathering receive and experience grace?

The ecclesiastical tradition of my youth is now the ecclesiastical tradition of my late-middle age. It suggests (and by "suggests" I mean that this is a creed we all sign and agree to uphold and defend) that there are two means of grace directly connected to all worship: preaching and the sacraments. Whenever someone is baptized, or whenever someone remembers their baptism, it is a grace to them. Whenever someone receives communion, they are receiving grace. And when a preacher proclaims the good news of Jesus, this can be, by faith, a grace.

Friends who began a new congregation in a university town put it like this: "We want attendees to receive grace every week. We hope they receive it in the liturgy; we hope they receive it in the sermon"—they suggested this was the weakest link—"and we believe they will receive it in the Eucharist. For a worship leader to believe such acts do offer grace—and we might argue that includes other acts too, such as the call to worship and the passing of the peace and the benediction—is to have a certain bearing. It is to believe, among other things, that worship leaders don't need to be especially charismatic or intelligent or naturally quick-witted or handsome or insightful but must simply point as clearly and directly as they can to the good news of gospel grace.

This has a profound effect on worship. For one thing, it vastly reduces the obvious or hidden pressure worship leaders feel to be superstars and instead encourages them to trust the ancient treasures of the liturgy to communicate grace. It's a paradox: the very act of pointing to the means of grace rather than at oneself may actually make one seem more charismatic or intelligent or naturally quick-witted or handsome or insightful. To keep pointing to grace is to live in the astonishing, life-giving reality of grace.

To live this proverb is to believe that worship by its very essence has grace built in. It's to know, in the deepest sense of knowing, that with faith it is impossible to worship *without* experiencing grace, even if it's mostly experienced subconsciously. Sometimes I overhear attendees ask after a worship service, "What did you think of worship today?" To shift from an evaluative critique of "What's in it for me?" to trusting that God will meet us in the sacraments is to live with a new kind of freedom. Worship less centered on individuals—particular personalities and moods and doubts and aspirations—and more trusting of the tradition (classic ordo) framed for mission is to have a grace-receiving bearing. To trust and rest in her baptismal identity means a worship leader need not strong-arm people into believing or experiencing certain emotions but can instead trust and delight in the God who gives grace.

Imagine the effect this emphasis could have on children and adolescents who attend services regularly. In a world with endless conflicting expectations about their appearance and performance and future, they might grow into adulthood believing and living the miracle that grace is a gift to receive. Imagine how living this proverb might enable worship to be a means of grace even to worship leaders themselves. Imagine approaching a service free from the need to be clever or innovative or wise, instead exuding, "I'm here to love you."

One small way this book can be a gift for worship leaders is by using it encourage each other to revel in the life-giving truth that the timeless worship practices are in themselves a gift for your congregation and for you. Imagine living week to week and hour by hour free from the tyranny of performance. Sure, a rise in adrenaline will be a part of the worship-leading experience for human leaders. But imagine leading with what John Calvin called *repose*. Envision leading worship with your full self, with gospel joy and abandon, but without having your identity at stake. Leading (and framing) with such a bearing will make worship more clearly a gift to you, and in living your calling with your inner narcissist out of the way, you might be more completely able to offer its innate gift to others.

Times I witness and remember that in worship we *receive grace:*

- When a worship leader pours water into a basin and the leader and congregation speak responsively about their baptisms, past or future, and their baptismal identity

- When a congregation confesses their sins and receives assurance

- When a worship leader uses a branch to fling water into the congregation (This is a long-standing practice in Orthodox congregations. I recently saw an Orthodox bishop sprinkle water in this way at an outdoor groundbreaking, to his—and the worshipers'—great delight.)

- When congregants of multiple generations and races walk forward to receive communion together (Recently one of our deacons said through tears, "I never get tired of serving communion. It's great every time!")

- When children delight in receiving grace—in baptism or communion

- When a worship leader is caught off guard by the emotion of a song and moved to tears

- When a congregation opens their hands and raises their arms in expectation as they receive a blessing spoken by their pastor or worship leader (One friend, a retired Baptist preacher who leads a men's group in our church, told me that at a recent gathering attendees said unanimously that the blessing was their favorite part of a worship service [a small part of me hoped a few might say it was the sermon])

- When an individual or congregation sings with joy and abandon (A few years ago an elderly man came to worship after his wife of fifty years died. As we sang our first song, I greeted him: "I'm so sorry about your loss, but I'm glad you're here." He responded with something surprising: "I have her here with me." He had an urn wrapped to his chest like a baby in a carrier. All this happened while our congregation sang "He gives and takes away; he gives and takes away . . .")

Worship celebrates and lives beauty.

Some longtime worshipers and worship leaders act like longtime married spouses who no longer see the beauty in the person they married years ago. Such spouses go through the motions of marriage but no longer seem to delight in those motions. They cease to see beauty in their spouse as a particular image bearer of God. Part of the call of worship leaders is to help worshipers, both secular novices and long-established veterans, to see the beauty around them.

Sometimes beauty seems obvious in worship. You enter a worship space where its soaring heights take your breath away. You listen to a well-trained choir sing the best of English hymnody at Westminster Abbey and marvel that you are in the 1,400-year-long line of worshipers who have heard this song. A string quartet or a sweet electric guitar inspires. A skilled tenor sings a familiar spiritual, and a congregation responds in full voice.

Other times, though, beauty needs to be mined from long-hidden places. In our Minnesota church was a family with three preschool boys. Their parents took them to worship faithfully, every Sunday morning and almost every Sunday evening as well. A few times, especially in the evening service, the preschoolers sat in the front row. I use the word *sat* loosely. What really happened was they lay on the floor between the front row of chairs and the pulpit. As their pastor (yours truly) did his best to convey the gospel according to the text of the day in his second sermon of the day, they lay in front of me (and the entire congregation), taking turns screwing their faces into entertaining expressions and giggling in response. Eventually they started rolling back and forth.

What could be the beauty in that? A wise worship leader might point out that at least they were there!

Beauty is intrinsic in Christian worship. It's there at every service, every week, in every setting. Grace is inherently beautiful. As a recent college graduate I led worship services in a campground amphitheater at Mount Rainier National Park. We sat on giant logs cut in half, and, when the cloud cover allowed, we had dazzling mountain views. One Sunday a visitor, noticing our *a cappella* music, asked if she might play an instrument she brought. I looked and saw she held an elaborately painted handsaw and bow. Knowing almost any instrument would raise the aesthetics far beyond my singing ability alone, I acquiesced. "Amazing Grace" never sounded so sweet.

James Schall describes attending the first public Mass celebrated in San Francisco's new cathedral in 1970. Just back from Europe and experiencing the great cathedrals there, he feared he might be underwhelmed by this new structure. But instead he was swept up in its beauty. When protestors suggested the money used for the cathedral would be better spent on the poor, Schall responded that the idea was and always will be "wrong-headed." He says, "One of my favorite themes has been that the 'Poor need beauty even more than bread'" and that to "offer the poor bread but not beauty is a high point in dehumanization."[3]

---

3. Schall, *The Praise of 'Sons of Bitches,'* 6.

An essential part of a worship leader's calling is to see this beauty and to help others see it too. Framing historic worship elements, like framing a Rembrandt or a Picasso, helps beginner and longtime worshipers alike experience the beauty already there. Again, wise worship leaders who know the historic worship elements are timeless treasures feel less burden or anxiety about *creating* beauty. They simply need to point to what is undoubtedly beautiful—baptism, Eucharist, blessing. Such a bearing understands there is beauty in all worship and in every neighborhood. A slogan of two friends planting a church in Oakland is "celebrating and cultivating beauty in our neighborhood." Their assumption: beauty is there, and their job is to help us see it and grow it.

The wise Apostle Paul encouraged every believer to focus on "whatever is true, whatever is noble, whatever is right, whatever is pure, whatever is lovely, whatever is admirable—. . . anything [that] is excellent or praiseworthy."[4] He lifted the list from famous virtue teachers and philosophers of his day. His encouragement can be specifically applied to worship leaders. It's easier, and sometimes more obvious, to see what is wrong and broken. There's something to lament every day and every week. But the call to see and point to beauty takes nothing away from lament as an essential feature of worship. It is wisdom for worship leaders (like Jesus) to announce and revel in the coming kingdom of God.

When I was growing up, our congregation had a pastor who was wonderfully gifted at pastoral care. Forty years after his departure, every subsequent pastor is still measured by his legendary pastoral effectiveness. As a high school senior I had surgery (a modest operation, really) for an ingrown toenail. My toe was important to me, more so because I was playing soccer at the time, but the procedure was fairly minor. He visited me! But the pastor was less gifted at leading worship. Every week he prayed a prayer—as children we called it "the long prayer"—that named every ill or grieving person in the congregation. The prayer also always included this line: "Lord, there is not a sound spot in us. From the crowns of our head to the soles of our feet we are sinners." Forty years later my family members can still recite it. What if he had instead framed a prayer for celebrating and cultivating beauty?

A pastor friend recently returned from a summer-long sabbatical. I was delighted to attend the first worship service on his return. He reported to his congregation, at the groundbreaking for a new facility, that during the summer he visited with expert tradespeople in Florence, Italy, who would design and build their marble fountain, craftsmen from Crete who were

---

4. Phil 4:8, NIV.

already busy making candles for them to use in liturgy, and those in New York and around the world who would be designing their mosaics. Their congregation had journeyed a long way from its earliest days of worship in a living room and then a storefront. Soon they will worship in a sanctuary that frames every historic part of their worship in architectural and artistic beauty. Sometimes the beauty of their worship is in 1,700-year-old (or brand-new) words, a prayer, or a liturgical response. Other times their wordless frames are offered by the long-practiced use of incense, icons, mosaics, music, and art.

Several years ago a Harvard English professor named Elaine Scarry wrote a fascinating book called *On Beauty and Being Just*. In a world where philosophers ask, "Have we become blind to beauty?" and where thoughtful people wonder if beauty distracts us from important issues and masks elitism, Scarry contends that beauty steers us toward what is truly important, like justice. She says that beauty *transfixes* us. In the presence of beauty we no longer think of ourselves as the center of the universe, but we are profoundly aware of others and, we would say, the Other.[5] Over the years I've seen aesthetics do what logic sometimes cannot: enabling someone, at times even the most hardened intellectual, to move toward grace.

Times I witness beauty in worship:

- A Navajo pastor serving for decades in a nearly deserted outpost in New Mexico, leading a congregation in celebrating communion even after their building is purposely burned[6]
- A grade-school brother and sister passing each other the peace
- A husband and wife in a season of bitter, ongoing disagreement passing the peace
- An adolescent playing guitar as worship leader
- A child reciting from memory a biblical text for the call to worship
- A new drummer exploring faith while playing music
- A person celebrating communion for the first time in her life

Worship can be intelligible to spiritual skeptics.

Our group sat around a dining table. Some familiar and some new to each other, we soon enjoyed the easy, free-flowing conversation of trusted friends.

5. Scarry, *On Beauty and Being Just*, 112.
6. "Fire Damage, Uncertainty in Days Following Arson."

We delighted in the food and celebrated a milestone, a friend's ordination into ministry. We swapped stories about favorite vacation destinations, the current geographies of our adult children, and specific challenges of our work lives. At one point the conversation veered toward the way Christian faith is lived—or not lived—in various parts of the country. One couple, thoughtful and dedicated believers, relayed a story about their child's college professor. While leading a conference in a highly secular California city, he had been out for a walk exploring the area. When he saw two women about to enter his hotel, he naturally held open the door for them so they could enter before him. He did it intuitively, just as he had hundreds of times in his Midwest hometown. But their reaction stunned him. Without breaking stride, one of the women glared, "We don't need a [expletive] man to open doors for us." The professor relayed this story as a reason he would not and could not live in California. The storytellers at that genial dinner relayed it as another item on their growing list of reasons to move out of California. Who could live among such secular people? My heart sank. I sat dumbfounded as the conversation swerved in another direction. What would it take for such solid, steady, thoughtful Christians to wonder together how worship in their congregation might be hospitable to those apparently secular women and their friends?

So far, the tallest person I have baptized is six foot five. An Ivy League master's graduate, Andy grew up outside any faith. When his sister-in-law read about our church, she told her sister, Andy's wife, "I think Andy would like that church." He did. Six months after his arrival, Andy ventured into volunteering on our sound and technical team. Then he joined a small group. A few months later he volunteered to teach children's ministry. It was then we told him, "It's best if you actually believe the lessons before you teach them to children." He agreed. He had too much integrity to simply go through the motions. So began a conversation that led to his baptism. Andy is unfailingly kind and polite, but like the women who declined the offer of a door held open, Andy was thoroughly secular.

One of the miracles of our congregation is that secular people worship with us. For thirty years an essential bearing of our worship leaders is to be *for* secular people. That doesn't mean we always agree with them. Nor does it mean our worship is first of all about them. It simply means we expect them to be present. We believe a good gift we can offer them is to introduce them to the timeless treasures of worship. So we frame worship with them in mind.

The denomination that birthed and nurtured my faith and to which I still belong is not known for winsome evangelism or for a long history of church plants adeptly reaching secular people. So it has regularly looked outside itself for sage advice from those who seem culturally bilingual, able to speak both Christian and secular.

A few decades ago, when I was beginning full-time pastoral ministry, veteran leaders invited young pastors to a conference to grow in mission ability and sensibility. Frustrated with our collective inability to reach people outside church walls, the denomination's missional leaders had invited a denominational cousin, the Rev. Robert H. Schuller, who at that time had a worldwide following for his *Hour of Power* television show. I admit my motives for attending the conference were mixed. The conference was in Southern California, and at the time I was a pastor in Minnesota. And the conference was in January. But I also was taken by what I took to be the original desire of Schuller's ministry: to frame worship in a way that the gospel would be intelligible to secular Californians uninterested in anything remotely connected to ordinary church.

A decade later, denominational leaders invited us to another conference, this one hosted by a Schuller protégé of sorts. Pastor Bill Hybels had been raised in our collection of churches, though he made it very clear he was no longer one of us. His Chicago-area ministry was attractive to our leaders in part because he was a native son who seemed able to frame worship (some might say *redesign* worship) to engage people with no Christian background or vocabulary.

The frontier ordo that strongly influenced our congregation's worship in the earlier years of our existence was shaped by these and similar conferences and conversations. But over time, I found myself personally longing for the treasures of historic worship. I felt like I was missing something. Was it just me, or was everyone in our church missing something? Was innovative worship in the best interest of my neighbors who didn't speak Christian?

A cynic might retort, "You're only going back to your particular worship and ecclesiastical tradition that was never really comfortable with frontier ordo." Fair enough. But I'm not first of all talking about going back to the tradition of my upbringing, though I see some wisdom in that. Rather, I'm inviting people back to and into *the* tradition, the worship equivalent of what C. S. Lewis called "mere Christianity," the worship treasures at the center of the Christian tradition.

About that time, together with a peer group of church planters, I attended yet another conference ("conference" might be generous; there were only twenty people gathered) at Redeemer Presbyterian Church in New York City. There we visited with and listened to Redeemer's founding pastor, Tim Keller, and its staff. All of us, tempted by models of ministry more innovative and pioneering, were taken by the winsome way Redeemer framed the vintage worship elements to be intelligible to secular people.

The congregation had found a way to both give space for secular people and invite them to the deepest treasures of the faith. What we win them *by* is what win them *to*.[7]

My hunch is that these stories seem dreadfully dated to you. That's on purpose. If you're still reading, hear me out. Whenever a congregation chases relevance, it will always feel dated in a short time. To pursue relevant worship is to start a race you can never win. You simply run round and round. Still, worship that is hospitable to secular people need not be as fleeting a fashion as leisure suits or Elton John's 1970s stage outfits.

Years later, I still appreciate the frontier ordo. I salute its aims. I value its sensibilities. It's just that, after trying it for more than a decade, I'm now convinced it isn't optimal for making the gospel intelligible to spiritual novices. A few years after our church started, one of my neighbors attended. We talked about sports, compared jobs, shared alcoholic beverages, and water-skied together (actually *he* skied; I involuntarily drank a lot of lake water, often at twenty-five miles an hour). After attending worship several times, he stopped coming. When I asked what he thought about our congregation he replied, "I like you. And I like the people there. But it didn't feel like church to me." My first reaction was, "You haven't attended church your entire adult life. What do you know about how a worship service should *feel*?" (No, I'm not defensive. And don't tell me I am!)

I believe the best way to reach people like Andy and my skiing friend and possibly the two women who scolded their volunteer door opener and the secular people in your neighborhood is to invite them to participate in the worship elements my neighbor craved—to offer these historic treasures framed in a way that is understandable to guests with no Christian memory or vocabulary. Even if such secular people are not yet present, even if their seats are empty, a worship leader speaks or frames as if they are. This is not to say worship is about them. It's not. It is to say we want worship to be intelligible to them. This is what Paul talks about in 1 Corinthians 14.

Framing is a basic Christian kindness. Framing worship is one way to honor people who do not yet believe as fellow image-bearers of God and as dearly loved friends and family of those who already believe, husbands and children and great-grandmothers. It is to welcome the great-grandmother who regularly attends our congregation and once told me with a sly smile, "I don't believe a word you say, but I like how you say it." It is to be hospitable to people who don't share our beliefs.

---

7. Over the years I have read and reread Keller's simple paper "The Missional Church," carolinechurch.net/adult/missional-church.pdf.

A friend born in the Netherlands told me such talk reminds him of the Dutch idea of hospitality. Their word is *gastvrijheid*. It literally means "freedom for the guest." It is never coercive, never demanding, but always designed to cultivate an environment in which the guest (in this case, the novice worshiper) can flourish.[8]

Times I witness and celebrate worship that is intelligible to Christian outsiders:

- When musicians carefully select songs with lyrics intelligible to both longtime attendees and spiritual rookies

- When ushers and greeters recycle pamphlets and paraphernalia needlessly placed on entryway shelves and tables because they are off-putting to secular people

- When a preacher speaks about doubt with tenderness and understanding

- When a worship leader reads (or better, recites) an entire psalm, even the dark and disturbing parts, in a worship service

- When a youth leader treats doubt as a sacred mystery

- When a mission-oriented community begins a new congregation in a highly secular neighborhood despite knowing they will likely always be small in number

- When a musician plays an offertory that appeals to church outsiders

Worship connects worshipers to global brothers and sisters.

Our modestly sized suburban congregation has people from two dozen countries of origin. A Filipino attendee told me her dad was part of the horrifying Bataan Death March of World War II. A Chinese attendee worries about his family still living in China. A Swiss attendee once gave me his perspective on global migration: "It's great to be born in Switzerland and to live in the United States." A Latina attendee informed me last week, "I go to the Roman Catholic church on Saturday night, but I want my children to attend here because we understand you." Several South African families started attending two years ago and come almost weekly. Another couple moved to our neighborhood from Cambodia. One of our youth leaders immigrated from Asia as an adolescent; another's grandfather is a Hmong shaman.

8. Thanks to Tim Blackmon for pointing this out.

We don't prioritize a global emphasis in worship because of these attendees. We prioritize the global identity of the church because of the creed that confesses one "holy catholic church." Wise worship is custom to a neighborhood. As soon as a congregation picks a language or music style, worship becomes local. But it need not be parochial. The New Testament revels in the way the gospel breaks boundaries between people groups.

While teaching a seminary class on spiritual disciplines, I illustrated memory's powerful role in identity formation by spontaneously starting to sing the Canadian national anthem. The class was held in the United States, but instantly the Canadian students, a minority, burst into song with me, swelling with an enthusiasm and pride that surprised even them. It was as if they levitated as they sang.

All through the Bible God identifies God's self as the God of *all* people groups. All nations come to him (Pss 47 and 72). Abram is renamed Abraham, the father of many nations (Gen 17). While Israel is God's chosen nation, the identity is not designed to promote ethnic pride or privilege, but to be a call to represent and extend God's love to all peoples. Every ethnic group and each nation has a place in God's geography. Consider the contrast: In Homer's classic Greek tales, Ethiopians are mythological figures, the stuff of tall tales, people uniquely loved by the gods who join them for parties. They live long and enjoy exotic diets. But the Bible treats Ethiopians not as myth, but as a people loved by God, those who will one day bring God special offerings (Zeph 3:9–10). Isaiah tells us that in God's amazing grace, at the end of time, when Jesus returns to make all wrongs right, nations and people won't lose their cultural identities. They will have them redeemed, swept up into the new heaven and new earth (Isa 66:18–19).[9]

Included on Jesus' family tree is Ruth the Moabite, Rahab the Amorite, and Bathsheba, the wife of a Hittite. Jesus talks extensively with a Samaritan woman. Is it no accident that we read about his disciple Philip explaining the gospel to an Ethiopian eunuch, or that a Roman centurion says after Jesus' death, "Surely this man was the Son of God."

I wonder what this multilayered cultural affirmation has to say about the kind of music we use in worship: Hip hop? R&B? Classical? Spirituals? Japanese folk tunes? Might it get us thinking about how many languages we speak? And what about symbols in our worship space? Do we honor one nation with one flag? Do we display a flag for every birth country represented in our congregation? Or might a thoughtful congregation display a flag from every country in which there is a church, or accent mission by

---

9. See Bauckham, *The Bible and Mission*, and Mouw, *When the Kings Come Marching In.*

displaying one from every country in which there is not yet a church? And how does one preach with an awareness of the way God treasures and designs all peoples?

Worship with a global outlook needn't foster a loss of cultural identity. Our cultural identities are renewed and redeemed in Christ. Paul tells the Colossians that in Christ they have put on a new self: "There is no Gentile or Jew, circumcised or uncircumcised, barbarian, Scythian, slave or free, but Christ is all, and is in all."[10] Worshipers may be slave or free. They may be Greek or Jew. They may even be Scythian. Scythian?

The ancient Greeks had one term for all non-Greeks: barbarians. But Scythians were the most barbaric of the barbarians. They were uncivilized savages. The ancient writer Flavius Josephus said they were "little better than wild animals."[11] (It reminds me of some middle schoolers I once knew.) One commentator says Paul intended "barbarians" to describe those from the south of Greece and "Scythians" those from the north, along what we call the Black Sea. Even Scythians belong; they too, with their language and culture and favorite beverages, can be swept up in the gospel story.

Worship need not flatten our national or cultural identities. The missional hope of the Bible is not to wipe out nations, but to celebrate their unique treasures. In worship we remember that we, with our particular languages and cultural experiences and countries of origins, are put at the center of this new community called the church. We are a new people. Together. All of us. No matter what our country of origin, we are now part of a new race.

David Bailey models and lives this every day. Years ago he determined that he didn't just want to talk about crossing ethnic and racial boundaries; he wanted to live it. So he formed Arrabon, a ministry that mentors the upcoming generation in writing and performing music and in crossing boundaries. Set in Richmond, Virginia, the former capital of the Confederacy, Arrabon is a kind of "artifact," a living embodiment of the vision of the new heaven and earth described in Revelation. It's no wonder then that Arrabon's "music ranges from Hispanic folk tunes and choruses in Urdu ("Jalali Yesu," or "Almighty Jesus") to funky neo-soul arrangements of familiar songs like the Doxology and Indelible Grace's "By Thy Mercy."[12]

How do you worship globally in your congregation? That is an adventure for you to discover. Our congregation consists mainly of native English speakers. Occasionally we sing in Spanish or Swahili or Korean. But in our

---

10. Col 3:11, NIV.

11. Mason, ed., *Flavius Josephus*, 10:321.

12. Shellnutt and Moody, "David Bailey."

framing and music we remind ourselves regularly (and celebrate) that even in a balkanized world where race and politics and ethnicity vie to be our main identity, we worship the God who loves all people. We belong first to the group Jesus calls out to be his church, a community that spans all times and all places, one that includes people from every continent.[13]

Times I witness worship connecting worshipers to their global sisters and brothers:

- When a worship leader leads a congregation in prayer for Christians of another country

- When a thoughtful musician includes a congregational song from another ethnic or language group, possibly one from our neighborhood

- When a musician like David Bailey gives his life to understanding his neighborhood and teaches young musicians to do the same

- When Arrabon or a North American congregation sings songs in Spanish or Urdu

Worship is timeless and historic.

One of the reasons our congregation has become so bullish about praying and often singing psalms in worship is that the psalms hold in tension many of the truths essential to worship leaders and the art of framing.

We see how psalms spiritually form us. They prepare us for times of grief. They prepare us to give thanks. They prepare us for times of lament. After 9/11, while writers of *The West Wing* scrambled to put a special episode together, our worship leaders scrambled to find lyrics appropriate to sing in a worship service. There were precious few in our repertoire. What we had were bits and pieces of psalms.

We see how psalms are hospitable and, in their unlikely way, intelligible to spiritual novices and doubters. Psalms understand that faith is more often like a winding country road than a level highway or well-plotted urban street. They teach us to pray the mess of what we feel, what we doubt, and what we believe and hold dear, even when we don't feel the psalms' exact pain or share their doubts at the exact moment we pray them.

We can also see how psalms teach us to pray with the global church. Our neighborhood might be ready to celebrate a humming economy and low unemployment, but our neighbors in Australia or Zimbabwe or

13. Adapted from Adams, "Scythian Worship?"

Hungary might be grieving a mass shooting, an eroding public trust, or a loss of safety.

Psalms are personal. We can pray them individually. But they are always shared, belonging to the community of the global, historic church. When we pray the psalms, we never pray alone. When we pray the psalms we are always part of the global (not just the parochial) church. This can be a new thought even for people familiar with Christian worship. Recently I was in conversation with a thoughtful twentysomething believer who grew up in the church. He's well versed on many faith subjects, but he found this idea surprising and new. He had never thought about it, but found it captivating: whenever we pray the psalms we are not praying alone, but with the historic church.

A few years ago a friend of mine and his wife had recently moved to a new urban center. After twenty-five years of ministry in a church they began together, a church flourishing in almost every way, they had launched into a new season of ministry, one that delighted them and leveraged their profound gifts for ministry: training new missional leaders. Then my friend started to experience some mild but persistent stomach discomfort. He was sure it was nothing, but at his wife's insistence, he made a doctor's appointment. His doctor gave the prognosis: pancreatic cancer. The next days and weeks were a scramble of tests and hospital visits and expert diagnoses, sometimes conflicting. But then he heard those fateful words: untreatable, inoperable, terminal.

For fifteen years, five pastors, including me, had met every Thursday morning at his instigation. The official purpose of our gathering began as accountability—a description none of us favored. Instead we grouped together for camaraderie and laughter, storytelling and problem solving, heartfelt prayer and simply being together—ordinary pastors living in the great company of pastors who have gone before.

Three of us drove the hundred miles to our friend's new apartment. There, on his eighteenth-floor balcony, we continued our camaraderie and laughter, heartfelt prayer and being together. We told stories, too, but we knew there would be no problem solving. Not this time. Only a month after that first doctor's visit, he was noticeably weakened. His words were few and softly spoken. We prayed, and we shared communion. As he received the body of Christ he paused, mid-swallow, as if hearing angels sing.

The next day I made a return trip with the fifth member of our ensemble. Unable to visit the previous day, he was intent on saying goodbye. Twenty-four hours later, a single glance told us our friend's end was near. At his family's gracious invitation, we gathered with them around his bed. He was past speaking. So, keeping vigil, we spoke for him. All of us—his dearly loved wife, his adult children and their spouses, and two pastor friends—recited words we knew from church. Formed by timeless and historic worship, we recited words we had learned: familiar psalms, much-loved prayers, and time-tested songs of abiding faith. For hours we sang from memory, one song after another, poignant moments interspersed with laughter that wondered if he even liked what we were singing. We did this until he passed—and heard the angels singing.

We left that day sober and grieving, but also grateful to have known a person of such sterling and contagious character. And we left, my friend and I, marveling at a family that knew what songs to sing from memory at their loved one's death bed. We found ourselves wondering which of the songs we sing in worship give a family words to sing at their father's dying.

There is a timeless way to worship just as there is a timeless way to build buildings. A recent podcast suggested pastors who start new congregations should think about how they can last at least three generations. Worship leaders can do that too. No matter our specific sub-tradition, we can vocalize truths from a historic and timeless tradition. The particular songs we sang at my friend's dying may not be for everyone. Some might even find them parochial. But together with the psalms, they were beautiful gifts to a dying man and his family.

We sometimes live the timeless reality of worship by designing frames that quote Christians who have gone before, who belong to every branch of Christianity—people like Augustine, Teresa of Avila, and Martin Luther King Jr. That is one reason theological education can be a good gift. It helps you know and enter into the center of timeless Christianity. Training in the timeless practices, the old ways, along with learning in and at and from a local church, is a stellar combination. Of course, timeless tradition needs to be applied, lived, and framed in fresh ways or it will ring hollow. Some worship leaders vainly go through the motions. People sleepwalk through the liturgy in every section of Christianity. That's why we encourage lifelong learning.

When we encourage designing frames that honor the deep wisdom and tradition of the church, we are inviting framers to go on a lifelong discovery about worship and the endless weekly applications. None of us ever really *arrives* as a Christian or as a worship leader. I'm struck by the self-proclaimed maturity of church attendees and leaders who have worshiped for decades, and maybe been part of church leadership for decades, but whose outlook is as calcified as a petrified forest. Worship practices, and the worship itself, is fossilized. Musicians and speakers appear robotic.

Worship is not something we master. You can get a master's in worship or a doctorate in liturgy. You can feel accomplished after several years or decades of leading worship in the same congregation. But there is always more to learn—infinitely more. And the learning fuels vitality.

The congregation of my childhood presented many opportunities for such learning: morning worship, evening worship, youth group, Sunday school, catechism, Christian day school. Much of that learning led to an event we called profession of faith (think confirmation, but at a time decided by each individual rather than at a specific age or grade in school). Once we made profession of faith, a beautiful thing, we were released from all further church education. We no longer needed to attend Sunday school or catechism classes. There was some clear incentive in that practice. But quite unintentionally, the long-standing practice of those robust and earnest Bible believers assumed that someone in high school had learned enough. This wasn't true. It never is. We understood precious little about worship, for example. But it gave the impression our faith had *arrived*.

Imagine instead a worship service of historic worship elements led by lifelong learners, endlessly curious about worship. Imagine services where doubting is expected and candid conversations about its reality are encouraged. Imagine a worship service in which leaders assume *all* attendees, not just spiritual novices, have a faith that is very much in process and is on a pilgrimage. Last summer I led a worship service at a conference and prayed before a sermon, "Lord, our minds are prone to wander, and for most of us, they have already wandered while sitting in this service." A Roman Catholic worship leader from Southern California was struck by the unflinching honesty. I was just praying. A historic worship element, the pre-sermon prayer of preparation, had new life.

Contrast wooden, dead, "we-have-all-*arrived*" behavior with a vision of worship as liturgical catechesis. Leaders who know they're not just passing people information, but are inviting worshipers into a deep and fruitful experience, believe worship liturgy is of utmost importance. Joseph Wagner, OSB, a proponent and practitioner of liturgical catechesis, says it "should allow the grace of God to work through the words, actions, and meaning of the liturgy in order to form our lives. It would thus transform us into little Christs to serve the church and the world."[14] Exactly.

Times I witness and celebrate worship as timeless and historic:

- When worship leaders dedicate themselves to being catechists as well as worship leaders
- When framing includes references to a saint (local or global; Protestant, Catholic, or Orthodox)

---

14. Wagner, "Liturgical Catechesis."

- When a congregation sings or reads an entire psalm together
- When someone reads a book on worship (like this one!) and starts a conversation
- When a family knows what songs to sing as a loved one lies dying

Worship is local, and new every time.

Erin Rose was in Charlottesville the weekend of August 2017 when, at a white nationalist rally, dozens were hurt and three people died. Erin, a worship leader and teaching pastor at East End Fellowship in Richmond Virginia, works with David Bailey, who also lives in Richmond and directs Arrabon.[15]

David recalled, "There had been a white supremacist rally in Charlottesville that May and a Ku Klux Klan rally in July—all to protest the city's plans to remove a statue of Robert E. Lee."

Erin added, "Clergy from all over the country had gathered to march in peaceful protest on Saturday against the white nationalist rally. I'd been asked to help with music at the Friday night service to cover the entire situation in prayer."

The service was packed. "There were six hundred people," Erin said. "Even the 'bigger name' people were so kind. The service was smooth and joyful, the prayers beautiful, and God was glorified. As we got ready to sing the last song, a musician got word that white nationalists were at the [University of Virginia's] Rotunda, across the street from the church. We sang "This Little Light of Mine" at the top of our lungs, clapping and stomping. Then we got word that men had surrounded the church with lighted torches. The police said we had to stay inside. . . . It felt unreal. They let the white folks out first. We couldn't leave till the marchers had moved to the university lawn."

After the Friday scare and Saturday violence, worship and sermon plans had to change. And they did. Rose was scheduled to preach Sunday night. David Bailey was already booked to preach at a majority-white church on Sunday morning. David says, "We talked a lot about how to preach about evil. Talking about racial reconciliation isn't all kumbaya. We have to acknowledge powers and principalities and people who allow themselves to be used for evil."

---

15. For more on Arrabon, see arrabon.com/what-is-arrabon/.

Erin says, "The proximity of Charlottesville to Richmond was jarring. This could have happened in Richmond, which was the capital of the Confederacy. I completely changed my sermon. We do that at East End Fellowship when tragedy rocks our city or nation. People depend on us to plan worship that helps them process the hard things. My attention always returns to how the church responds to divisive events. God has reconciled himself to us, so we as churches are called to lead in reconciliation."[16]

In the ongoing chaotic aftermath of Charlottesville, Bailey and Rose acted with the same skill as those "Isaac and Ishmael" writers, directors, and actors from *The West Wing*. They lived the best of the Christian worship tradition. The gave voice to the lament and gospel hope of their community, worshiping in a way both fresh and specific to one local congregation and faithful to God's work in every congregation over the global centuries. They framed and lived worship for mission.

This work of framing worship is historic and current, timeless and timely, like that *West Wing* episode, the wise work of Erin and David in Charlottesville, or the worship you lead in your neighborhood.

16. Story and quotations from Huyser-Honig, Bailey, and Rose, "David Bailey and Erin Rose on Charlottesville, Violence, and Preaching."

"*Existence has greater depths of beauty, mystery, and benediction than the wildest visionary has ever dared dream. Christ our Lord has risen.*"

—Frederick Buechner, *The Magnificent Defeat*

One thing I ask from the Lord,
this only do I seek:
that I may dwell in the house of the Lord
all the days of my life,
to gaze on the beauty of the Lord
and to seek him in his temple.

—Psalm 27:4, NIV

The Spin Room, Sincerity,
and Witness to Beauty

IF THE FIRST 2016 presidential debate between Donald Trump and Hillary Clinton wasn't spectacle enough, further theater (as one reporter said, "the real show") happened afterwards, in the spin room. One by one, devoted backers of each candidate appeared in the massive space to hype their nominees and "play promoter for the horde of gathered reporters."[1]

The first post-debate spin room was created in 1984 by the campaign of then-President Ronald Reagan. Campaign officials appeared after the debate, speaking on the record, playing up Reagan's successes and minimizing those of his Democratic rival, Walter Mondale, even though many expert observers believed Mondale had just won the debate. That first unabashed and unapologetic attempt to claim debate victory despite evidence to the contrary was christened "spin patrol." Four presidential elections and dozens of spin rooms later, a tactician for the 2000 Al Gore presidential campaign described the savvy and ultimately winning spin of their opponent's team. Skillfully working their message, the Bush side played up the post-debate picture they wanted viewers and pundits to remember most: a condescending vice president. Over and over, they highlighted Al Gore's exasperated sighs. "They beat us after the debate in the spin room," strategist Tad Devine told *The New York Times*. "Their spin was, 'He lied and he sighed,' and that took hold."[2]

In the spin room, a wide range of characters appears, all promoting their candidate and very likely themselves. Nearly everyone says the same thing in their own different way: "My candidate won."

When I told a friend about this book's subject, she responded straightaway, "Are you going to talk about the dark side of framing, our human

1. Frizell, "Presidential Debate Spin Room."
2. Calderone, "For 2012 Presidential Debates, Campaigns Speed Up the Spin."

temptation to spin things to benefit us and make us look good?" I hadn't yet considered framing in those (dark) terms. Her insightful question stuck with me: Does the very act of framing (or worship leading in general) tempt even the most devoted and sincere worship leaders to focus some facet of a worship frame (or worship leading in general) on themselves? In a crooked twist of sin, might the very act of leading worship offer a built-in, almost-irresistible opportunity to promote oneself? In the very moment an adept worship leader highlights an enduring worship treasure, are they also drawn to display their own cleverness, even their own sincerity? Veteran worship leader and spiritual formation guide Henri Nouwen wrote, "I have realized more and more that even my seemingly most spiritual activities can be pervaded with vainglory."[3] Speaking of his career as a priest and professor, including times of leading worship, he added, "There is a great temptation to make even God the object of my passion and to search for him not for his glory but for the glory that can be derived from smart manipulation of godly ideas."[4]

How do we avoid turning worship leadership into our own personal spin room, a "post-debate circus where both candidates' allies fight to have the last word and define the all-important narrative of the night"?[5]How can we frame worship to genuinely honor God rather than ourselves and lead worship with authenticity and sincerity?

We begin by exploring what it means to be sincere. Sincerity may be the unending desire of our generation. Worship leaders and worshipers focus repeatedly on soul-searching questions like: Are we sincere? Is our worship sincere? Are our songs and prayers authentic? How can I be certain of my own sincerity as a worship leader? Worship leaders often harbor such inner doubts even when congregants collect around such leaders, acting and speaking as adoring fans: "Isn't our worship leader clever?" "Isn't she winsome!" and "Doesn't she just absolutely make the Bible come alive?"

In a superb article on worship and sincerity, liturgical specialist John Witvliet writes that the plea for sincerity was a "central concern of the Protestant Reformers, a concern that intensified in subsequent centuries as Puritans, Pietists, Quakers, and Revivalists doubled-down on attempts to codify or re-ceremonialize liturgy, and promoted their own rituals of sincerity and spontaneity." Church history, he continues, overflows with "soul-searching exploration and liturgical experimentation" designed to cultivate and ensure sincerity. Over the years worship leaders (and worshipers) have wrestled

3. Nouwen, *The Genessee Diary*, 70.
4. Nouwen, *The Genessee Diary*, 70.
5. Frizell, "Presidential Debate Spin Room."

with "the difference between . . . prescribed liturgies and free prayer, pairing rubrics and models for extemporaneous prayers." Witvliet calls sincerity in worship "a centerpiece of many liturgical movements over the past thirty centuries," adding that "among my mostly Protestant students, no theme is more contested, misunderstood, or cherished."[6]

The Apostle Paul talks about his conduct among the congregation at Corinth as having "integrity and godly sincerity."[7] Later he remarked that, "[u]nlike so many," he did not "peddle the word of God for profit" but instead spoke "before God with sincerity, as those sent from God."[8] Considered in this way, godly sincerity is "clearly a noble virtue that bridges the gap between belief and conduct. It signifies a certain wholeness and consistency, a lack of foreign alloys."[9]

So understood, it seems remarkably wise to celebrate and promote sincerity. But we are wise to promote it with a wary eye. Philosopher James Schall warns that contemporary people (he was writing in 1978) believe sincerity itself has a kind of saving power. So in the name of sincerity people march blindly on, assured that "what God wants to know is not what we have done or what we have believed but rather whether we were authentic and honest and sincere with ourselves."[10] He goes on to warn, "in the ways it is used these days at least, sincerity is more probably a vice. But if it must be a virtue, certainly it must be the most dangerous one about."[11] To prove his point, he reminds us that Adolf Hitler's vision for a reborn and flourishing Germany was exceedingly sincere.

During Schall's tenure as a professor at the University of San Francisco, a Jesuit school, administrators passed a new edict requiring all Roman Catholic students to attend several classes about their faith. After all, they reasoned, students should understand how their faith informs their thought and life. In response to this attempt to nurture a sincere understanding of faith in them, scores of students declared themselves non-Catholic, so dodging the new requirement. It makes me recall the pre-marriage counseling session I had with a young engaged couple. One soon-to-be spouse declared he was a dedicated Christian while the other stated clearly her complete lack of interest in anything religious. In response, I verbally relayed an inner hesitancy to marry people so blatantly unmatched in faith and outlook. In

6. Witvliet, "The Mysteries of Liturgical Sincerity."

7. 2 Cor 1:12, NIV.

8. 2 Cor 2:17, NIV.

9. Schall, *The Praise of 'Sons of Bitches,'* 63.

10. Schall, *The Praise of 'Sons of Bitches,'* 62.

11. Schall, *The Praise of 'Sons of Bitches,'* 62.

good conscience I could more easily marry two agnostics together or two Christians together than one of each. The professed Christian responded instantly, "Well, if it makes you able to continue as our wedding officiant, consider me an agnostic. I'm happy to be considered one."

Sincerity is complicated—more complicated than we wish. An overly heightened emphasis on sincerity becomes a form of self-absorption. "Sincerity," Schall says, "is concerned first with ourselves, with how *we* relate to ourselves. It is essentially ingoing. . . . [It] always needs a touch of vanity."[12]

Instead of making sincerity our central aim, Schall advocates for what he calls "civility." Sincerity might tempt worship leaders to bare their souls to a congregation as a mark of authenticity: to share their recent grim medical prognosis, to relay this morning's argument (fight?) with their spouse, or to report the secret concern they have about the new senior pastor's general competence. Civility, by contrast, "demands that on frequent occasions your first loyalty is not to the unfettered expression of your own sensations, feelings and desires, but to other principles such as tolerance, respect, and even love of your neighbor."[13] Civility requires you speak a kind word even when you're angry. You love a neighbor, even though she is of another political persuasion. You change a child's diaper, though you'd rather keep your hands clean. Civility obliges people to do what is right and good rather than what is comfortable or true to themselves. Civility may require us to write frames for worship or lead a worship service at the exact moment we would much rather be sitting in our favorite café drinking chai tea and delighting in a new novel. By contrast, "The only thing left when we are sincere with ourselves is ourselves."[14] Even a reflection on sincerity might in part be self-promoting and insincere.

In addition, Witvliet points out, "Operational definitions of sincerity vary widely across cultures, centuries, philosophical frameworks, and Christian traditions." Sincerity "subtly dawns on the stolid faces of Danish fishing villagers in *Babette's Feast* and erupts in expressive cries in Korean *Tongsung Kido* prayer." Some congregations nourish strong emotion in their worship leaders; others believe it is an unwanted distraction. Some assume extemporaneous prayer "the purest form of sincerity" and others as "hubris that is at once dangerous and ineffective."[15]

Applying the slippery demands of sincerity to a worship frame, we might overhear ourselves speak a frame designed for the Lord's Prayer:

12. Schall, *The Praise of 'Sons of Bitches,'* 65.
13. Schall, *The Praise of 'Sons of Bitches,'* 68.
14. Schall, *The Praise of 'Sons of Bitches,'* 68.
15. Witvliet, "The Mysteries of Liturgical Sincerity."

These are very likely the most repeated words in human history. Already today Jesus' followers have prayed them in cathedrals and in storefront churches, in glittering urban centers and in desperate slums. Let's pray them now, joining with the church around the world and through the centuries.

You may then proceed to speak Jesus' timeless prayer along with a congregation only to find yourself *feeling* inauthentic. While speaking, you notice you feel tired and cranky, even irritable. Then you remember your deep-seated worry about the current chaos in your church's leadership and the bitterly divided vote happening immediately after today's service. Next you discover yourself calling to mind specific people who this past week worked artfully and diligently to thwart your good intentions and sully your reputation. The honest-to-God truth is that right now you'd rather be watching football than leading a congregation in prayer. In the face of such a reality, is it sincere to continue? In the name of pure sincerity, should you stop praying and relay your thoughts completely and honestly to your unsuspecting congregation? Such truth-telling comes with a risk: will sincerity inspire them to proclaim in solidarity their own wandering thoughts, or will they bury their own tangled emotions while declaring you unfit for worship leadership?

In our world of spin and spin rooms, where for decades Roman Catholic high officials dodged the real-life trauma of children, where a popular megachurch pastor steps down for illicit behavior and then retracts his confession three weeks later, and where secular people fiercely suspect all faith is a con game, is *all* worship spin? How can anyone trust words spoken by a person framing worship?

I propose three (framing) mind-sets to move worship toward sincerity as a virtue.

First, imagine yourself as a worship colleague with the great "cloud of witnesses" described in Hebrews 12. The previous chapter in Hebrews celebrates a pantheon of saints for their faith and faithfulness. Individual believers are held before us as inspirations. But anyone who knows their background stories finds the shining presentation bewildering. Each all-star is an unruly mess. One gets drunk. One deceives. One murders. All stumble in living their faith. To focus on sincerity among these faith forerunners: Was Noah sincere when he drank excessively after pressing his first post-flood wine? Was Abraham sincere when he told the kings of Egypt and of Gerar that Sarah was his sister? Was Jacob sincere when he snookered his father? Was Moses sincere at the burning bush when he said, "What if you send my brother Aaron instead?" Was David sincere as he wrote poems about doubt and trust and imploring God to smash his enemies? If they were entirely sincere, they were often sincerely wrong.

Still, even if those who make up the cloud of witnesses are flawed, consider the benefits of cultivating a mind-set that remembers these spiritual ancestors are part of your worship leadership team. A "cloud of witnesses" mind-set reminds us that whenever we stand to lead worship, we do not stand alone. We stand in the great company of those who have gone before us and are to come after us. And in such company we know that while the validity of any Christian worship is aided and made more readily believable by sincerity, it does not (thank God!) rise and fall by in-the-moment sincerity. The cloud of witnesses as a community authenticate the truth (more on that later) of what any one individual is saying at a particular moment.

As I write this section I'm sitting in a Trappist monastery, on a retreat with church planters. My fellow leader and I hope to offer these pastors and their upstart congregations a sense of identity that doesn't ebb and flow with the immediate circumstances of their local ministry's success or failure. And, bright people that they are, they want to receive this gift. They actively seek ways to unhitch their ego from a congregation's varying moods. One thoughtful retreatant, noticing the elderly bearing of most of the monks in the Abbey, asked, "How does a monk think about chanting the same three psalms (4, 91, 134) during the Compline service that ends every day?" Do the math. If you chant the same three psalms every night for forty years, you've nearly chanted them 15,000 nights in a row. The church planter continued, "Does a monk find that repetition gets boring? Or does it enrich his experience over time?" In this new communal mind-set, we might ask, "Does it matter?" If a monk receives and lives his identity as part of a cloud of witnesses via a Benedictine tradition that goes back to the sixth century and the broader Christian tradition that goes back to the apostles, maybe his own personal reaction doesn't matter so much. Knowing his place in the throng of witnesses, he can be free from fretting about his inner sincerity and free to focus on the One he adores.

Aided by monastic visits like this, I am increasingly intrigued with the spiritual formation implications of holding in mind this image of the great cloud, or company, of witnesses. Nouwen, that much-loved writer on spirituality, considered this cloud of witnesses during a sabbatical stay at this same monastery. He said his academic life had barely "any room for the saints." (Most Protestants find that true, whether on purpose or by neglect!) But in the monastery, "saints are like roommates with whom you can have long conversations."[16] What if worship leaders routinely consider

16. Nouwen, *The Genessee Diary*, 73.

themselves *roommates* with the great cloud of witnesses who have gone before? Conversation with roommates from the global church would make
any frantic focus on measuring or affirming or hiding one's own personal
sincerity evaporate—or at least diminish. That energy could be redirected
(freely) to focus on glorying God himself.

Yesterday I spoke with Brother Christian, a monk who has been at
this Abbey more than fifty years. During Nouwen's sabbatical stay, they
worked closely together, digging boulders for use in constructing a chapel
and working side by side in the bread factory. Talking with Christian made
me feel closer to Nouwen. This unassuming ninety-year-old wasn't aware
that our rambling conversation was connecting me to the great cloud of witnesses. Or maybe he was. But spending time with this ecclesial roommate
helped me remember again that our congregation's experience of the holy
doesn't rise and fall on my sincerity or skill.

This is not a plea for insincerity or a condoning of erratic or spiritually destructive behavior. Corruption in the church reminds us that church
discipline is also a needed grace. But in bringing to mind the great cloud of
witnesses, the thorny worship questions birthed by my particular Christian
tradition seem less pressing. Inner critiques that impulsively rise toward
those who experience (sincere) worship in a different form fade to silence. I
feel less need to question the sincerity of those who kiss icons, or raise hands
and sway, or ad lib communion liturgy, or sing lyrics I deride, or repeat a
psalm 15,000 nights in a row. After all, we're roommates.

This idea, to focus on the company of witnesses, is an old one. John
Chrysostom wrote about the Eucharist, "The angels surround the priest.
The whole sanctuary and the space before the altar is filled with the heavenly Powers come to honor Him who is present." And elsewhere: "Think
now of what kind of choir you are going to enter."[17]

A prayer from *The Book of Common Prayer* begins:

> We praise thee, O God: we acknowledge thee to be the Lord.
> All the earth doth worship thee: the Father everlasting.
> To thee all Angels cry aloud, the Heavens and all the Powers therein.
> To thee Cherubim and Seraphim: continually do cry,
> Holy, Holy, Holy, Lord God of Sabaoth;
> Heaven and earth are full of the majesty of thy Glory.
> The glorious company of the Apostles: praise thee.
> The goodly fellowship of the Prophets: praise thee.
> The noble army of Martyrs: praise thee.
> The holy Church throughout all the world: doth acknowledge thee;

17. Danielou, "The Presence of Angels at the Eucharist."

> The Father: of an infinite majesty;
> Thine adorable, true: and only Son;
> Also the Holy Ghost: the Comforter.[18]

It's far more difficult to overdeliberate or fret furtively over one's deepest inner motives after beginning a prayer like that.

A second mind-set to cultivate sincerity as a virtue is to remember our call to *witness*. Witnesses need not (completely) embody the truth; we point to the truth. Witnesses need not set a perfect example, but direct people to the One who does.

A witness knows sincerity is not binary. Sincerity is not like an on/off switch. It's not that most worship leaders are either sincere or not, either genuine or not. It's more often, as we've been saying, that worship leaders are a tangle of sincerity. We live and lead with a mess of jumbled motives and wounds and aspirations. A witness need not worry primarily whether they are personally "on" or "off"; rather a witness keeps pointing to the One who is all sincerity. Sincerity, like all of virtues (and all of life), is better considered as an ongoing direction than a realized destination. Our personal sincerity ebbs and flows, but our unchanging priority is to point each other to the truth of Jesus. Even before a worship service when a leader feels particularly unfit for ministry, the call to witness remains.

Here again we can consider our friend Benjamin, the verger at Westminster Abbey. It is a good and beautiful thing that he (from outside appearances) *loves* his job. Watching him sashay among the treasures housed in that centuries-old building could spark a cynical visitor to startling joy. Even so, Benjamin is well aware that he is not (and never needs to become) the focus of Abbey guests. He is a witness. He points to the beauty there—the Abbey history, the inspiring lives of those buried inside, and the many treasures of the British people. He may be charming and winsome and even charismatic, but more than any or all of these qualities, he is a witness who points to the fundamental purpose of the building in which he leads tours: to promote the life of a worshiping community.

One of the pastors I have most admired in my life is the Rev. Charles Greenfield. Rev. Greenfield became a pastor during the Great Depression of the 1930s. During his seminary days, a classmate once asked a professor what they should do if a parishioner asked them an especially difficult question. The professor advised, "Those situations accent why a pastor should smoke a pipe. You can light and relight your pipe, stalling for time as you think of the right answer." Rev. Greenfield's first parish was a fairly new congregation in rural North Carolina. The congregation housed him in a parsonage with

---

18. "Te Deum Laudamus," *The Book of Common Prayer* (1662).

walls that couldn't keep out the wind, with floorboards that couldn't cover the dirt below, and with a plumbing system that couldn't keep out aquatic species. (He told me that the moment they first turned on the faucet at the kitchen sink, a fish came out.) One of my relatives described Rev. Greenfield saying, "He's as common as an old leather shoe." This declaration, spoken by a blue-collar admirer, was intended as a huge compliment. Other pastors they had experienced were overly formal or brimming with words only for the most educated. Some pastors in that congregation preached with a kind of preacher's tone that no one would use ordering food at McDonald's. An old leather shoe, indeed. Rev. Greenfield was sincere. At his retirement he returned to our congregation: it was home. Over the years, Rev. Greenfield officiated at my parents' wedding, my grandfather's funeral, and my ordination to pastoral ministry.

Charles Greenfield was from a different era. He could never be "Pastor Chuck." But formal nomenclature did not diminish his ability to relate to a common person. He was not perfect. I was too much his younger (fifty years) to know his particular foibles. I do know about the day someone asked if he was going to take a call to leave his current congregation and move to a different one that had asked him to become their pastor. He responded, "I'm still praying about it and not yet sure." Fair enough. But the wry storyteller who first reported the conversation pointed out that Mrs. Greenfield was already upstairs packing up the bedrooms for their impending move. Rev. Greenfield's comment that day didn't diminish his authenticity. It seemed to add to it. The congregation didn't need him to be a perfect person or a perfect worship leader. They needed him to be a witness. And he was.

It's a treasure when a worship leader is a witness who both lives and tells the truth, both moment by moment and over a lifetime. It's a gift to know people like Rev. Greenfield and have them in your life. The gospel truth is more readily believable if the one presenting it is truthful and trustworthy. But even a selfish person can be a witness. In a passage that has always troubled me in my own desire for authentic Christian leaders, the Apostle Paul describes leaders who preach (and, we might assume, lead worship) "out of selfish ambition, not sincerely." Further, he says, such self-aggrandizing persons seem intent to "stir up trouble for me while I am in chains." These people are exactly the opposite of the Rev. Greenfields of the world. Rather than be dismayed, Paul remarks, "But what does it matter? The important thing is that in every way, whether from false motives or true, Christ is preached. And because of this I rejoice."[19] Apparently, the gospel is so resilient even a scoundrel can be a witness.

19. Phil 1:15–18, NIV.

The third mind-set: Sincerity grows as a virtue when a worship leader points to beauty. We witness *to* beauty.

British television regularly portrays vicars. Characters range from the three mad priests in *Father Ted* to G. K. Chesterton's murder-solving *Father Brown* to the handsome rookie vicar in *Grantchester*. The sitcom *Rev.* features actor Tom Hollander as the Rev. Adam Smallbone. Adam is a Church of England priest who moves to the small (in attendance) inner-city church, St. Saviour in the Marshes, a socially disunited parish in Hackney, East London. Loath to shut the church to anyone, Adam juggles the needs of everyone: those experiencing homelessness, substance abusers, sincere devotees, and upwardly mobile parents using the church to get quality education on the cheap.

In the neverending challenge and mess of local ministry, a jumble he seems ill-suited to face, Adam manages week after week to witness to beauty. He sees God's hand in the mundane and ordinary lives of his unorthodox churchgoers. He sees with hope. He speaks with kindness. He treats people—all people—as if they bear the image of God. Adam is not perfect. He can be weak when he should be strong. He can yield to temptation or be intimidated by the wrong things. Still, he is a witness. His mind-set is to be a witness to beauty. Nearly everyone writes off his parishioners, even the overbearing archdeacon who seems to make Adam's life more miserable. But through the chaos Adam points anyone who will listen to the beauty within them and the beauty of what Jesus has done for them.

We all serve at our own St. Saviour of the Marshes. In our very specific settings, we are called to point people to see again (or for the first time) the timeless beauty of the One we worship.

Charles Spurgeon wanted his congregation to share the same experience. Sounding like the venerable and vivacious nineteenth-century minister he was, he enthused in his commentary on Psalm 27:4:

> *"To behold the beauty of the Lord."* An exercise both for earthly and heavenly worshippers. We must not enter the assemblies of the saints in order to see and be seen, or merely to hear the minister; we must repair to the gatherings of the righteous, intent upon the gracious object of learning more of the loving Father, more of the glorified Jesus, more of the mysterious Spirit, in order that we may the more lovingly admire, and the more reverently adore our glorious God.[20]

Beholding the beauty of the Lord is the one thing, says Spurgeon, "which, if a Christian had, he needs desire no more." For those who love God, it "is

20. Spurgeon, *The Treasury of David*, vol. II, 3.

enough even to satisfy us, the fruition of God, and the beholding of him . . . to have correspondence and fellowship and communion with him there."[21]

Worship leaders witness to the Beauty who is the source of all beauty. And they do it chiefly as a witness to the beauty in worship elements that point to the beauty of the Lord.

Throughout this book I advocate that this is best done via the historic liturgy. We might also say it can be most *sincerely* done via the historic liturgy and vintage liturgical elements. For example, there is missional beauty in the Eucharist as it rehearses the life-giving work of Jesus, invites people to feast at his table, and nourishes their souls. There is beauty in baptism: Imagine a young woman overwhelmed with the anxiety that frequently comes in a world that burdens us with custom-designing our own identities and building lives that prove we are valuable. The woman hears the liturgy of baptism that says "In Christ you are my beloved child," and she remembers her identity and value are a divine gift. There is beauty in passing the peace between generations and people estranged. Imagine during a hotly charged presidential campaign a right-wing Republican and devoted Democrat reach across the (church) aisle and say with great feeling and sincerity, "The peace of Christ be with you." In a world of spin there is great beauty in the confession of sin: An adolescent's peers tell him repeatedly, "It's *your* life, you can do whatever you like." But through the historic liturgy he regularly confesses his own contribution to the mess of the world, working a spiritual muscle that will build a lifetime of integrity. Rather than being burdened with the pressure to be novel or captivating or to design spiritual moments, a worship leader relying (with a beauty mind-set) on the beauty of a historic worship element simply need witness, trusting the time-tested liturgy to do its graceful work.

As Adam Smallbone reminds us in his fictional parish, living our calling to witness to beauty in the enduring worship elements nourishes our ability to witness to beauty in the specific circumstances of people in our neighborhood: the husband who takes his wife with Alzheimer's to worship faithfully each week, the teenager who makes room for his autistic brother to sit beside him, the usher who makes space for a wheelchair user.

Sincerity is nourished as we witness to beauty.

Reflecting on our retreat at the monastery, one missional leader said, "I've been in paid ministry for twenty-five years. My bosses over the years loved me because I got stuff done. However, I slowly ground down to a shell of myself. I lost a huge amount of my humanity and had a breakdown. I was collapsing under the weight of being a successful pastor and executive

---

21. Spurgeon, *The Treasury of David*, vol. II, 8.

director. Our time at the monastery renewed me." We might again say: to be a witness to beauty.[22]

The point is not that you need to visit a monastery (though that may be true), but that you need to be in a place where there is no spin—and become the kind of person in whom there is no spin. Not even by you. A monastic invitation tells potential retreatants that, like everyone else, the brothers go through periods where they are excited about prayer and times when they are not, but no matter how they feel, they go to the Divine Office. Such a practice helps a monk get outside himself and learn to offer his own desires and feelings to God. A wise (sincere) worship leader, like a monk, is a witness to beauty freely given: in silence, psalms, passing the peace, Eucharist, and benediction.

Worship may seem miles away from the spin room. But worship leaders, a bit like presidential candidates at times, are sorely tempted by spin. Famous people may not be singing our praise, but we often we are (even if unconsciously) looking for votes. What if instead we witness to beauty?

"The spin room," writes one reporter, "is a place where nothing gets resolved and no battles are won. . . . But sometimes there is no spin in the spin room. Like when Mark Cuban was asked whether he'd run for president as a Democrat or a Republican. 'I'm not running for president,' Cuban said as he power-walked toward a television interview. "You think I would go through this bull****?"[23] His response was disarmingly sincere.

Worship leaders share his logic. Most don't want to sign up for such a complicated and challenging (and sometimes thankless) task. No spiritually healthy person chooses to lead worship simply to gain attention, flaunt their intellect, or fill up their schedule. The only reason to take such a job, the only reason to work so diligently to frame and lead worship, is that you're called, surrounded by the great company of those who stand with you. You can think of no other way to live than as a witness to beauty.

22. Thanks to Joel Kiekintveld for allowing me to share part of his reflection.
23. Frizell, "Presidential Debate Spin Room."

Bibliography

Adams, Kevin. *150: Finding Your Story in the Psalms*. Grand Rapids: Faith Alive Christian Resources, 2011.

————. "The Gospel in a Handshake." *Reformed Worship* (blog), July 30, 2018. https://www.reformedworship.org/blog/gospel-handshake.

————. "Scythian Worship? Nations and Cultures at Worship." *Reformed Worship* (blog), July 7, 2015. https://www.reformedworship.org/blog/scythian-worship-nations-and-cultures-worship.

————. "Shaping a Congregation's Worship DNA." Workshop at Calvin Symposium on Worship, Grand Rapids, January 27, 2017.

"Barth in Retirement." *Time* 81, no. 22 (May 31, 1963) 35–36.

Bauckham, Richard. *The Bible and Mission: Christian Witness in a Postmodern World*. Grand Rapids: Baker Academic, 2004.

The Book of Common Prayer. Cambridge: John Baskerville, 1662.

Bruney, Gabrielle. "The *Game of Thrones* Showrunners Are Ready to Talk About That Coffee Cup." *Esquire*, September 2, 2019. https://www.esquire.com/entertainment/a28890270/game-of-thrones-benioff-weiss-coffee-cup/.

Calderone, Michael. "For 2012 Presidential Debates, Campaigns Speed Up the Spin." *HuffPost* (blog), October 1, 2012. https://www.huffpost.com/entry/2012-presidential-debates-spin-room_n_1929185.

Chesterton, Gilbert K. *Orthodoxy*. London: John Lane, 1908.

————. *What's Wrong with the World*. New York: Dodd, Mead, 1910.

Cherry, Constance. *The Worship Architect: A Blueprint for Designing Culturally Relevant and Biblically Faithful Services*. Grand Rapids: Baker Academic, 2010.

Corrigan, Kerry. "Advice to My College Freshman." *The New York Times*, August 13, 2019. https://www.nytimes.com/2019/08/13/well/family/advice-to-my-college-freshman.html.

Craughwell, Thomas. *Saints Behaving Badly: the Cutthroats, Crooks, Con Men and Devil Worshippers Who Became Saints*. New York: Doubleday, 2006.

Cyprian of Carthage. *The Unity of the Church*. In *Ante-Nicene Fathers*, Vol. V, edited by Alexander Roberts and James Donaldson, 423. Edinburgh: T&T Clark, 1885.

Danielou, Jean. "The Presence of Angels at the Eucharist." *Catholic Exchange*, September 25, 2018. https://catholicexchange.com/the-presence-of-angels-at-the-eucharist.

Didascalia Apostolorum. Translated by R. Hugh Connolly. Oxford: Clarendon, 1929.

"Fire Damage, Uncertainty in Days Following Arson." *The Banner* 154, no. 9, October 2019, 18.

Fosdick, Harry Emerson. "The Importance of Doubting Our 'Doubts.'" Sermon at Asbury Theological Seminary, Wilmore, KY, 1940.

Frizell, Sam. "Presidential Debate Spin Room: Where the Real Fun Begins." *Time*, September 27, 2016. https://time.com/4509051/presidential-debate-donald-trump-hillary-clinton/.

Granite Springs Church. *Worship Guide*. Lincoln, CA, 2019.

Gross, Bobby. *Living the Christian Year: Time to Inhabit the Story of God*. Downers Grove, IL: InterVarsity, 2009.

Healy, Michelle. "Were the Three Wise Men from China?" *USA Today*, December 30, 2010.

Huyser-Honig, Joan, Erin Rose, and David M. Bailey. "David Bailey and Erin Rose on Charlottesville, Violence, and Preaching." Calvin Institute of Christian Worship resource library, accessed October 4, 2019. https://www.christianitytoday.com/ct/2016/julaug/david-bailey.html.

Introduction to "Isaac and Ishmael." *The West Wing*, season 3, episode 1, originally aired October 3, 2001 on NBC, accessed October 4, 2019. https://www.youtube.com/watch?v=WSAMKvADVhg.

Johnson, Erskine. "In Hollywood." *Dunkirk Evening Observer*, October 20, 1949.

Johnson, Trygve. "The Altar Call of Hope: What My Campus Needs More Than Anything Else." *Reformed Worship* 88, accessed October 3, 2019. https://www.reformedworship.org/article/june-2008/altar-call-hope.

Keller, Tim. "Evangelistic Worship." New York: Redeemer Presbyterian Church, 2001.

King, Martin Luther, Jr. "Prayers." *The Papers of Martin Luther King, Jr.*, Volume VI, 137.

Lincoln, Abraham. "Letter to Mrs. Bixby." In *Abraham Lincoln and the Widow Bixby*, by F. Lauriston Bullard, 26–27. New Brunswick, NJ: Rutgers University Press, 1946.

Mason, Steve, ed. *Flavius Josephus: Translation and Commentary*. Leiden: Brill, 2007.

Mathetes. "Epistle of Mathetes to Diognetus." Translated by Alexander Roberts and James Donaldson, accessed October 4, 2019. http://www.earlychristianwritings.com/text/diognetus-roberts.html.

Merton, Thomas. *Praying the Psalms*. Collegeville, MN: Liturgical, 1956.

Mouw, Richard J. *When the Kings Come Marching In: Isaiah and the New Jerusalem*. Grand Rapids: Eerdmans, 2002.

———. *Uncommon Decency: Christian Civility in an Uncivil World*. Downers Grove, IL: InterVarsity, 1992.

Niebuhr, H. Richard. "Doubting Believers and Believing Doubters." Sermon at Spring Glen Church, Hamden, CT, April 28, 1957. bMS 630/2 (8). Papers, 1919–1962. Andover-Harvard Theological Library, Harvard Divinity School, Cambridge, MA.

Nouwen, Henri J. M. *The Return of the Prodigal Son: A Story of Homecoming*. New York: Doubleday, 1994.

———. *The Genessee Diary: Report from a Trappist Monastery*. Garden City, NY: Doubleday, 1976.

O'Brien, Tim. *The Things They Carried*. First Mariner Books ed. Boston: Houghton Mifflin, 2009.

Plantinga, Cornelius, Jr. *Engaging God's World: A Christian Vision of Faith, Learning, and Living*. Grand Rapids: Eerdmans, 2002.

———. *Not the Way It's Supposed to Be: A Breviary of Sin*. Grand Rapids: Eerdmans, 1995.

Plass, Ewald M. *What Luther Says*, vol. 1. St. Louis: Concordia, 1959.

Ross, Melanie C. *Evangelical versus Liturgical?: Defying a Dichotomy*. Grand Rapids: Eerdmans, 2014.

Sanneh, Lamin. *Whose Religion Is Christianity? The Gospel Beyond the West*. Grand Rapids: Eerdmans, 2006.

Scarry, Elaine. *On Beauty and Being Just*. Princeton, NJ: Princeton University Press, 1999.

Schall, James V. *The Praise of 'Sons of Bitches': On The Worship of God by Fallen Men*. 2d ed. South Bend, IN: St. Augustine's, 2019.

Shellnutt, Kate, and Andie Roeder Moody. "David Bailey." *Christianity Today* (online), June 23, 2016. https://www.christianitytoday.com/ct/2016/julaug/david-bailey.html.

Spurgeon, Charles. *The Full Harvest 1860–1892*, vol. 2 of *Autobiography*, rev. ed. Edinburgh: Banner of Truth, 1973.

———. *The Treasury of David: Volume II*. London: Marshall Brothers, 1881.

Stubbs, John. *John Donne: The Reformed Soul: A Biography*. New York: W. W. Norton, 2006.

Trinity Episcopal Cathedral. "Welcome to Trinity Episcopal Church: Information to Help Orient You." Trinity Episcopal Cathedral, Portland, OR, 2017.

Wagner, Joseph. "Liturgical Catechesis." *Church Life Journal*, October 3, 2017. https://churchlifejournal.nd.edu/articles/liturgical-catechesis/.

Warren, Tish Harrison. *Liturgy of the Ordinary: Sacred Practices in Everyday Life*. Downers Grove, IL: InterVarsity, 2016.

Witvliet, John. "The Mysteries of Liturgical Sincerity." *Worship* 92, May 2018, 196–203.

———. "Biblical Psalms in Christian Worship: Overlapping Scripts in the Unfolding Drama of Liturgical Performance." Kavanagh Lecture, Yale Divinity School, October 2012.

Witvliet, John D., and Carrie Steenwyk, eds. *The Worship Sourcebook*. 2d ed. Grand Rapids: Calvin Institute of Christian Worship and Faith Alive Christian Resources, 2013.

Index